The Ghost Tour of Great Britain

Nottinghamshire

The Ghost Tour of Great Britain

Nottinghamshire

with *Most Haunted's* **Richard Felix**

breedon **books**
PUBLISHING

First published in Great Britain in 2006 by
The Breedon Books Publishing Company Limited
Breedon House, 3 The Parker Centre, Derby, DE21 4SZ.

ISBN 1 85983 506 6

Printed and bound by Biddles Ltd, Hardwick Industrial Estate,
King's Lynn, Norfolk.

CONTENTS

ACKNOWLEDGEMENTS

The production of this book would not have been possible
without the help and expertise of:

the other members of the Ghost Tour team,

Steve Lilley and Delicia Redfern

Nathan Fearn

and all the staff at Breedon Books in Derby

LANDS
END
2003

NEW YORK 3147

JOHN O'GROATS 874

ISLES OF SCILLY 28
LONGSHIPS LIGHTHOUSE 1½

NATIONAL GHOST
TOUR

The Ghost Tour team (left to right): Steve Lilley, Delicia Redfern, Richard Felix.

PREFACE

When local historian Richard Felix opened a Heritage Centre in his home city of Derby, England, in 1992, even his far-reaching powers of perception could not have forecast how important a step he had taken.

The Heritage Centre, based in an area of the city known as St Peter's churchyard, became the starting point for Richard's innovative ghost walks and within 12 years more than 150,000 people – many of them so fascinated by the concept that they visited from America – had booked in to be scared out of their wits.

Soon the Derby ghost walks took on legendary status and were attended by scores of would-be ghost hunters. The story unfolds as ghost walkers leave the Heritage Centre and are told that they are walking over the bodies of many of the victims of the Black Death. They head down St Peter's Street towards the site of Derby's first gaol, a place of incarceration for witches, heretics and traitors. The Lock-Up Yard, the scene of the brutal murder of a policeman, is visited next. A moment's reprieve permits the ghost-hunters to partake of another kind of spirit in the Tiger Bar, in preparation for a subterranean trip down into the barrel-vaulted tunnels beneath Derby's Guildhall. The story continues as the party heads across the Market Place, then on to the Cathedral, the Shire Hall (the scene of a horrendous pressing to death in 1665), before returning to the Heritage Centre for a Ghost Hunter's Supper – for those who can stomach the feast that is!

With the success of his ghost tours in Derby it became clear to Richard Felix that a formula that worked so well in one place would probably succeed in other towns and cities across the British Isles, and so when he was approached by film producer Stephen Lilley to record a remarkable DVD series – *The Ghost Tour of Great Britain* – he jumped at the chance. It was a mammoth, time-consuming task that relied on the great British public taking the idea seriously. And they did. The intrepid pair visited every major city and well over 40 counties throughout England, Scotland, Ireland and Wales and, with incredible attention to detail, they attempted to uncover explanations for each eerie haunting, researching library archives and interviewing credible witnesses, historians, renowned psychics and parapsychologists.

As interest in the ghost walks and *The Ghost Tour of Great Britain* increased, so did Richard Felix's fame as an authority on all things paranormal. He was invited to become the resident historical expert on the hugely popular Living TV show *Most Haunted*. Appropriately, one of the places investigated by *Most Haunted* was Derby Gaol – undoubtedly one of the most haunted sites in Britain. Situated in the basement of 50/51 Friar Gate, Derby Gaol is a working museum where visitors can see the actual cells where prisoners were kept. It was used as a prison from 1756 to 1828 and, following its acquisition by Richard Felix in 1997, has been restored to its original condition. Now visitors can try paranormal investigations using the latest hi-tech ghost-hunting equipment, just as the *Most Haunted* team did on film inside the Condemned Cell. Those of a fearless disposition can even sign up for a Derby Gaol Sleepover, comprising a mini ghost walk for an hour and a half around Friar Gate, a pie and porter supper and a bar that serves all night! A medium can also be arranged to carry out séances and private readings.

This book has been written to accompany the DVD series and recounts in words and pictures the chilling accounts of paranormal experiences uncovered by Richard Felix and Steve Lilley on their groundbreaking trip, *The Ghost Tour of Great Britain*.

PART ONE

GHOSTS

AND HOW

TO FIND

THEM

RICHARD'S THEORIES ABOUT GHOSTS

As I was raised in a haunted house, you will forgive me for having well-formed ideas about the existence of ghosts. After years of study and countless fascinating experiences, some of them truly frightening, I now consider myself an expert in the paranormal.

It may surprise you to learn, therefore, that as a child the very thought of spirits, ghouls and skeletons filled me with fear and dread. I was petrified by ghosts and, to a certain extent, I still am to this day. When I was no more than four years old I was locked into garages and garden sheds by so-called friends and told that the 'Green Ghost' was going to get me. Experiences such as this only served to fuel an already fertile imagination and as a child I would refuse to stay in any building on my own and would certainly never walk past a churchyard alone or even walk upstairs without someone's hand to hold. I spent many a night as a youngster lying wide awake beneath my bedclothes, waiting for a demonic being to stride into my bedroom, pull back the bedclothes and reveal its hideous face. Of course this never happened, but perhaps my way of facing up to my fears was to attempt to discover all I possibly could about how and why spirits haunt places.

In the early 1990s I started to conduct ghost walks around Derby – and 12 years later well over 150,000 people had been on a ghost tour of my home city. Derby's location, almost in the centre of the country, has underlined its great importance for almost 2,000 years and contributed to its prosperity. It has always been a crossing of the ways and was the scene of the last hanging, drawing and quartering to be carried out in England, the result of the last rebellion against the Crown to take place in this country.

However, every region of these isles has its own folklore and legends and in recognition of this Stephen Lilley and I embarked on *The Ghost Tour of Great Britain*. In less than three years we visited nearly every county in the land, looking for ghosts, talking to people who have seen ghosts and visiting haunted places. My experiences as an expert on the popular *Most Haunted* TV programme have broadened my horizons still further and put me in direct contact with the scariest places in Great Britain and beyond. Even today, however, I am still learning and remain grateful to the

folklorists and parapsychologists who continually surprise me with their thoughts and theories.

In this book, you will read chilling tales of hauntings, but I will also attempt to pass on, from my own experiences, the knowledge and details of the equipment you need to detect paranormal activity yourself. In short, everything you need to know to become a ghost-hunter.

First, however, you need to understand what a ghost is.

Some parapsychologists don't believe in life after death and put hauntings down to the influence of the living, not the dead. They attribute unexplained events to Extra Sensory Perception (ESP) – the psychic powers of living individuals who have the ability, for example, to move objects.

We are taught from an early age that we *can't* do certain things. If a door opens by itself, a spoon bends without any force being applied to it or a glass on a mantelpiece suddenly shatters, as adults we look for a logical explanation. Those who believe in ESP say that this desire to explain away inexplicable events is no more than a safety valve – far better to be a sceptic than attribute strange happenings to the power of the mind and run the risk of being ridiculed. And at least ESP and the idea of telepathic understanding between living creatures is a more comfortable theory to swallow than the spectre of the dead being trapped on earth as punishment for terrible crimes or through the tragedy and pain of an unexpected demise.

The idea of sharing our world – sometimes our own homes – with the spirits of dead people is uncomfortable to say the least, but I have met hundreds of sane, sober individuals who swear they have encountered a ghost. Intrigued? Well, before you read on, please make a note of the Richard Felix Rules of Ghost Hunting. First, you have to be an enthusiast. Second, you need to be a detective, and third, most certainly a sceptic. You have to explore all avenues when you look into a ghost's history and get to the bottom of the *reason* for the haunting.

For many, that would be enough. However, I passionately believe the ultimate aim of the ghost-hunter is to ask: 'How can I help?' If you're looking for nothing more than the cheap thrill of a scary experience, go and watch a horror movie. I feel that there's a responsibility attached to ghost-hunting. If an animal lover tracks down a caged gorilla, does he simply take a photograph of the sad ape and walk away? No, that's not enough – the final act has to be to release the creature from its pain. It is therefore important to understand that ghosts – whether the product of the living or the dead – haunt places for different reasons and I believe that there are at least five distinct types.

The dead returning

This is where a spirit is seeking some kind of 'closure', as our American friends might say. It can interact, is aware of its environment and knows you are there – it's a conscious entity that can even speak to you. To me, this is the most frightening type of ghost, but what's the reason for its existence? The basic premise is that while the spirit of a dead person remains on earth, the soul moves on to its eternal reward. So maybe our interactive ghosts have business on earth they haven't concluded or are somehow trapped and can't move on to where good souls go.

In the Middle Ages there was a strong belief in Purgatory – a state in between heaven and hell. Quite often human bones are found where ghosts have been seen for a number of years and a common theory is that troubled souls haunt the earth because they weren't buried properly. The way we depart this life isn't something most of us think too deeply about these days, but in bygone times people craved a decent burial. Could denial of the Last Rites or bitterness that their bones were interred in ground that was not consecrated create the energy of a troubled ghost, stubbornly waiting for a proper burial?

I spoke recently to a Cornish woman who told me that through the Church's influence in the Middle Ages and its warnings of eternal damnation, souls that had done bad deeds in life were simply too afraid to move on, so instead hovered on earth as ghosts.

This theory may help to explain why we don't see many modern ghosts – there was more fear in the past of the punishment for sins in death, hence the reluctance of some to take the step into the afterlife. Perhaps these days we are more relaxed about our wrong-doings and don't believe they have to be paid for when we die?

Some ghosts apparently don't have any choice about whether or not they move on to another place. We have long been told that individuals who have committed terrible crimes are condemned to walk this earth for eternity, repenting their sins. Marley's ghost in Charles Dickens's *A Christmas Carol* warns Scrooge to mend his ways, or face the prospect of dragging in death the heavy chains he has forged link by link throughout his corrupt life.

The fact that these interactive ghosts represent the dead returning and the spirits of real people – entities with intelligence – makes them difficult to track down. Why would a self-respecting ghost with the ability to interact allow itself to be nailed by a gang of hi-tech ghost-hunters wielding laser temperature readers?

The apparition

If you could take a camcorder and video player back in time 200 years, imagine how staggered the people of early 19th-century Britain would be at your ability to play back on a screen a particular event you had just recorded.

So why are we shocked today by the idea of a traumatic event, perhaps a terrible premature death, somehow recording itself naturally into rock, brickwork, or even soil? Stone in particular is an ideal recording medium because it contains silica, and it's my belief that the energy emanates out of the stone.

I believe electronic impulses emanate from the brain in the moments before death takes place, creating energy that imprints itself into the fabric of the location. When atmospheric conditions are right, the image created by this energy replays the scene. That's why you see an apparition as it was just before the person died, but it's no more real than watching John Wayne in an old cowboy movie. The Duke long ago rode off into the sunset to that big ranch in the sky – it's his image you see and hear on video and it's impossible for him to interact with you. The same can be said for apparitions.

The tragic scene is played out again and again, but this ghost can't interact – there's no sense of the apparition being aware of the living. Just like a favourite videotape that is played too often, apparitions tend to fade through time. There are stories of ghostly hauntings that have become less distinct down the years, starting out, for example, as a red lady in the 18th century, changing to a pink lady in the 19th century, then to a white lady in the 20th century before becoming no more than a pillar of light accompanied by the sound of footsteps.

Telepathic projection

Like the apparition, this ghost is created by a moment of crisis. We've all heard stories of the woman who sees the image of her husband stranded on a mountain or a soldier appearing to his family moments before he is killed in the trenches.

These are classic examples of the telepathic understanding between people who love each other. In some cases the person who appears as a 'ghost' doesn't actually die, because their appearance prompts a loved-one to summon help. We have all experienced that nagging voice in our head that tells us to visit a relative or friend we know is sick. It's a telepathic experience linked to high emotion.

Phantasm

This is a bizarre apparition that, some would say, proves that ghosts are as much to do with the living as the dead. In the 1888 Census of Hallucinations, a huge survey, the Society for Psychical Research interviewed people throughout the British Isles and Northern France and came up with a surprising statistic. It was discovered that where those questioned were actually able to identify the ghost they had seen, half of the 'ghosts' were still alive and in no danger at the time they were seen! Phantasms are created by another form of telepathy, where an individual, though alive, somehow places an image of himself elsewhere. Far-fetched? Well I have a first-hand account of a baker who, after he had retired, was seen by the new owner of the business as an apparition going about his duties in the bakery. The new owner assumed that he had seen a ghost and that the old baker must be dead. However, on further investigation he discovered that the old man was very much alive, but had little to do in retirement. Consequently he spent most of his time in solitude, daydreaming about his old job. In doing this he somehow provoked the ghostly image of himself to appear at his beloved bakery to be witnessed by the new owner.

Poltergeist

Poltergeists represent a big group of ghosts. There are two contrasting schools of thought on exactly what makes a poltergeist. The name comes from the mediaeval German words *polte* (noisy) and *geist* (ghost). Once again the definition of this ghost comes down to a battle between the living and the dead. One side of the argument believes poltergeists are mischievous, sometimes malevolent, spirits who inhabit a particular place, often a room. The other side goes with the theory of Recurrent Spontaneous Psycho Kinesis, or RSPK for short. They believe that living people, for reasons we don't understand, use the power of their own minds to affect their environments.

Scary movies have given many people a very definite idea of what poltergeists do. We have been drip-fed an image of mischievous spirits throwing objects across rooms, but poltergeist hauntings tend to be more measured than the cinematic interpretation suggests. More regularly they start with a scratching sound and then move on to the odd loud bang, progressing to unpleasant smells. Eventually objects start to move – not initially by floating across a room, but in an annoying way. A set of house keys you always leave on the kitchen table disappears, you hunt high and low and half an hour later you find them – exactly where you left them.

Then come phenomena known as 'small object displacement'. Everyday objects disappear from a room and reappear in a different place. The next stage of a poltergeist haunting is that unusual items appear from nowhere. Old wooden toys, teddy bears, and, at its most grisly, human bones, have all been reported as appearing in rooms. Eventually poltergeist activity progresses to the classic image of objects flying across a room. It's interesting to note though that objects in these reported cases are said to float in straight lines, rather than going up and down in an arc the way they would if you or I threw something in the air and let gravity take charge.

I have very seldom spoken to anyone who has been damaged physically or mentally by ghosts – nor have I heard of poltergeist activity resulting in objects actually hitting anyone. I believe poltergeist activity isn't either mischievous or malevolent, but a call for help. The longest poltergeist incidence I have encountered is a year, but more usually it's a matter of weeks or months.

Filming one episode of *Most Haunted*, our camera captured a teddy bear flying across a room where a child had died many years before.

It seems that poltergeists focus either on a particular person or on a particular place. I have spoken to parapsychologists who have totally sealed off a room where poltergeist activity had been reported. They left a camera running and there was absolutely no possible way the room could be interfered with by any living being. They waited outside and within a minute heard a huge smashing sound. Running into the room, they found the camera pointing at the floor and a teddy bear, last seen on a sofa, sitting with its paws up in front of the fire, as if to warm itself against the cold.

Quite often, poltergeist cases seem to have a living agent. It's normally people who are highly intelligent, creative and imaginative, possibly disturbed by family issues. It is claimed that emotionally charged individuals troubled, for example, by the onset of puberty, cause some poltergeist experiences. That is why it is so important to map out family relationships and areas where an individual might be emotionally charged before diving in with theories and solutions. Where poltergeist activity results from one person's emotional state, the issue needs to be treated with sensitivity and respect. Sometimes a far more sensible alternative to chasing the poltergeist is recommending sound medical assistance.

A GUIDE TO GHOST-HUNTING

If you regularly tune in to the *Most Haunted* TV show, you'll see us using all manner of sophisticated ghost-hunting equipment. There really are some superb ghost-hunting aids on the market these days, and I'd advise you to examine these hi-tech units if you are looking to back up investigation successes with scientific evidence.

However, when starting out as a ghost-hunter you can, if you wish, get away with pretty basic equipment, much of it to be found around the house.

A **torch** is essential and **candles** are useful too because in addition to giving soft light they can detect movements and draughts. Another 'must have' is a **tape recorder** or **Dictaphone**. A useful rule with regard to taping sound is not to leave your recorder running – it's painstaking and ultimately unrewarding to listen back to hours of tape after a ghost-hunting session. Much better to use your tape recorder only when you have asked your ghost a question – such as the classic 'Is anybody there?' Then switch on your recorder and leave it on for two or three minutes and you could get some very good results.

You can get away with an everyday **thermometer** to gauge sudden drops in temperature, but better still is a **laser thermometer**, which detects the temperature at exactly the point its red scan light hits and gives a reading on a handheld gauge.

Tape – such as household masking tape – is useful for taping off areas of activity or windows. A piece of **thread** can also be useful to section off small areas, such as a tabletop.

To assist in monitoring the movement of trigger objects, items that move during poltergeist activity, an upturned **transparent case** can come in handy. Try a plastic fish tank – and I'd recommend an empty one! Putting trigger objects underneath plastic makes for a more scientific examination of item movement because it eradicates the possibility of anything being moved by natural factors, such as draughts or wind.

In the absence of digital recording equipment, something as basic as a piece of **graph paper** at least gives you the opportunity to map out items on a table or in a room before and after a poltergeist haunting.

Dowsing rods are ghost-hunting implements you need to acquire a relationship with, and a feel for, quite literally! In simple terms the rods are two pieces of thin rigid wire, the consistency of a typical Firework Night sparkler and around 18 inches long in each case. Place each rod lightly between the first and second finger of each hand and, with fists clenched and facing away from the body, and elbows slightly bent, hold the rods out horizontally in front of you approximately six inches apart. Try them out in any space, particularly one where a haunting has been reported, and simply ask the rods to give you 'yes' and 'no' answers to questions. I believe you get a 'yes' when the rods cross inwards and a 'no' when they angle away from each other. If you ask if a spirit is in the room you are in and the answer is 'yes', you can then ask the rods to point in the direction of the spirit. Patience and concentration is needed, but in my experience dowsing rods really do work. I don't know *how* they work but my gut feeling is that it's something to do with the power of the mind transmitting itself through the body and into the rods. Ask me for a scientific explanation and I can offer none, but my own personal experience of using rods is both positive and genuine.

If and when you really catch the ghost-hunting bug you might want to invest in some of the incredibly sophisticated pieces of state-of-the-art equipment now on the market. Such is the interest that there are companies such as the British-based Spectral Electronics that now deal exclusively in ghost-hunting aids.

The **Electro-Magnetic Field (EMF) meter** has been used for several years now by ghost-hunters and by paranormal investigators. This hand-held machine, not much bigger than a TV remote control unit, can detect electro-magnetic presence in the fabric of buildings; useful when investigating, for example, regular reported sightings of an apparition in the same place. The latest generation of EMF meters, developed specifically for paranormal investigators, are ingenious because they filter out everyday electrical charges such as mains frequencies. With a pair of normal headphones you can also measure variations in electro-magnetic energies recorded by the meter.

The **Ultra-Sonic Unit** is pretty new on the market. In look and feel it is similar to an EMF meter with a display and an audio connection. Ultra-Sonic Units measure acoustic energies in ultrasound regions at frequencies of 20khz and above, a range of sound that bats and, significantly, dogs can hear, but way beyond normal human hearing. Animals generally seem more sensitive to paranormal activity than we humble humans and devices such as the Ultra-Sonic Unit help us to redress the balance. Previously some ghost-hunters would take dogs on investigations because they seemed to be able to pick up things that humans couldn't. With the head-phone connection you can monitor high-frequency sounds and, if you wish, record them onto your Dictaphone. Some of the more advanced paranormal investigation groups have even developed computer programs that enable users to store and interpret information using sounds recorded through Ultra-Sonic Units. These programs are available as free downloads on the Internet and can display spectrum analysis ranges that show, for example, energies recorded in different frequencies. So Ultra-Sonic Units do so much more than simply replicating the sensitivity of dogs, and the real beauty of them of course is you don't have to take them out for walks!

The **Negative-Ion Detector** is another 21st-century phenomenon. The low-light infrared filming we carry out on *Most Haunted* often shows up orbs, small objects that seem to fly through the air like tiny flying saucers. These orbs are believed to have some relation to high voltage or static electricity, a side effect of which is a surplus of negative ions. You can create your own electro-magnetic field through the old trick of rubbing a balloon against a jumper, creating an energy that allows the balloon to stick to a ceiling. This is the same type of energy picked up by Negative-Ion Detectors, which give out an audible beep to indicate activity.

Interviewing technique is also crucial, despite the availability of modern-day equipment that can make the business of ghost-hunting easier and ultimately more exciting. Investigators of paranormal activity must be prepared to talk to people who have witnessed a haunting when amassing evidence. It is essential therefore to develop an effective interviewing style. Devoting hour upon hour of your own time to ghost stakeouts is all very well, but it is always important to factor in the experiences of other people who have personal accounts to tell of activity in a particular case. It is rather like a detective cracking a criminal case: having first-hand evidence is fine, but to prove your case you need to accumulate witness statements. For these statements to be as effective as possible, like a police detective, you also need to develop a good interviewing technique. Let your subjects do the talking, prompt them with open-ended questions and gently but firmly ask them to stick to the facts of what they have personally seen or heard, not what they have been told by others.

Always record your interviews on a tape recorder or Dictaphone. Ask permission of your subject first of course, and respect their privacy, but recording interviews is important because it enables you to concentrate not only on what is being said, but on the *way* it is being said. Our intuition helps us form an impression of whether someone is speaking sincerely or lying through their teeth. Witnesses' body language will often either give them away or underline their credibility. If you are convinced by the sincerity of your witness the next step is to listen back to the tape and make a full transcript. This is where you, as a detective, must take a sceptical view of the evidence. If a particular witness informs you, for example, that a door in a particular building regularly slams shut for no reason, then look for a logical explanation. Is the activity caused by a through-draught that occurs naturally when another door is opened elsewhere in the house? If a witness reports the smell of tobacco in a particular room at certain times and attributes this to the presence of a pipe-smoking ghost, could it in fact be more to do with temperature changes inducing an odour in paintwork, plaster or old floorboards? Could the sound of ghostly footsteps be nothing more sinister than your neighbours in the house next door, movement in the rooms above or even thermostatically controlled central heating kicking in with a rumble and a thud?

In Tutbury Castle there's a 17th-century costume presented on a shop window-style mannequin that appears to sway entirely on its own. In fact the room where this costume is displayed shares the same old floorboards as the adjoining King's Bedroom at the Castle. Although a partition wall was erected to make one room into two at some stage in the Castle's history, the effect of walking in the King's Bedroom moves the floorboards in the adjoining room and sets the mannequin moving!

Your most reliable witnesses will inevitably be people who live or work in the place where they report paranormal activity. They will be aware of everyday sounds that have a natural cause and will be able to speak to you with greater authority about happenings that are genuinely unusual. The problem with ghost hunts and people whose experiences relate to a location they are not familiar with is that every small sound or movement seems to demand an explanation. It's far better to rely on the witness statements of people who are truly familiar with the place where a ghostly presence is reported. Give particular weight to the statements of those witnesses who stick to the facts of what they have experienced rather than speculating as to the cause. If they tell you they regularly hear footsteps in the cellar followed by a loud bang, but haven't any idea what causes this phenomenon, it's a more telling observation than someone who goes on to speculate that the activity is probably caused by the ghost of an unhappy monk who hanged himself in the

15th century, because Mrs Jones in the village reckons the house was once the site of a monastery…

A **methodical approach** is crucial for ghost-hunting. Sherlock Holmes may be a fictional detective, but he was given a very factual philosophy on detection. When approaching a case he would rule out the impossible and examine what he was left with, as this, he believed, was the truth, however improbable that truth seemed.

I can testify from personal experience to the emotion attached to seeing a ghost at first-hand and the careful analysis I went through afterwards to convince myself of what I had seen. It happened in Derby Gaol, not at dead of night during a low-light ghost hunt, but in the middle of the afternoon in a kitchen when I was on my mobile phone in conversation with a friend. Through the open door of the kitchen I saw a figure, the size of a person and grey as grey, move down one of the old gaol's corridors. Although there was no drop in temperature, I sensed it as well as seeing it. By the time I got to the actual door to the corridor, it had gone.

This experience frightened me, quite a lot. However, when I recovered I then went through the process of ruling out all the naturally occurring things that might have caused its appearance. Although what I saw had a misty appearance, it wasn't smoke, it wasn't steam and it wasn't the reflection of a car's headlights. There's a theory known as 'Standing Wave' that tells us that in certain conditions extractor fans in rooms, corridors and even in computers can give off an odd acoustic effect that creates the impression of something moving fleetingly at the very edge of an individual's vision and prompts terrible feelings of fear and anxiety. However, the grey mass I saw wasn't out of the corner of my eye; it was a full-on experience and I can think of no other explanation than my having witnessed a ghost.

Here is something strange but true: while filming an episode of *Most Haunted* I saw a spoon fly through the air. I wasn't the first person to the errant spoon when it landed and my slowness off the mark on this occasion probably saved me getting my fingers burned! In some instances items subject to poltergeist activity, whether cutlery, coffee cups or other general household objects, have been found to be red hot to the touch. This I put down to the poltergeist energy created in its movement, so approach with care!

Continuing the methodical approach to all things para-normal, it is important to log examples of poltergeist activity for future reference, so always weigh the object that has apparently moved and measure how far it has travelled. This statistical information can help you prove, for example, that items of a certain weight tend to travel a certain distance in a particular room. At the very least it is information you can pass on for others to quantify. Organisations such as the Society for Psychical Research will always be happy to offer assistance provided you have facts and figures to support your questions.

Original artefacts are always good for measuring powers of perception through a simple touching and sensing test. Anyone can try it, though some, inevitably, are more sensitive than others. Here's what you do, in a group if you wish: lay the palms of your hands lightly on an artefact – anything from a sideboard to a sword – and then clear your mind completely. Try to register signals from the item you are touching; then talk about it.

Folklore is the development of history rather than hard historical fact. For example, it may be factually correct that in the Middle Ages a woman leapt to her death from the north tower of a castle after her knight husband returned early from battle to discover her with a lover. The folklore element is the tale passed down through the ages that the apparition of a white lady is seen leaping from the same tower just before midnight, or that a candle will never burn when lit in the room at the top of the tower.

So how, as a ghost-hunter, do you try to bridge the gap between folklore and fact? First, as always, gain permission from the owners of the property you intend to investigate. You may even feel it is sensible to have a member of staff of the haunted building – a curator of the castle for example – present throughout the investigation. At the very least, draw up a written agreement with the owners or trustees of the building that your investigation has been sanctioned. I would then devise experiments suitable to the environment and probably arrange a vigil where at least two people, armed with digital recording equipment, sit at the haunted site and quite literally wait for something to happen. The vigil might take the form of a small séance where you as the ghost-hunter invite spirits to make contact. Although you as the leader of this particular investigation will be fully aware of the folklore surrounding the site in question, it's probably a good idea that others in the vigil party know as little as possible and go into the experiment with few pre-conceptions.

Ensure too that **evidence** collected during the vigil is not contaminated by over-elaboration. If, for example, a member of the party sees the apparition of an old soldier walking through a wall, he should not turn to a colleague and ask: 'Did you see the old soldier walk through the wall?' The best response would be simply to ask: 'Did you see that?' The colleague then replies with a simple 'yes' or 'no', again guarding against over-elaboration that might later be construed as auto-suggestion. Importantly though, both members of the vigil should make a note of the time of the conversation and record exactly what they did or didn't see.

If you see a ghost-hunter seemingly poking himself in the eye in a moment of high excitement during a vigil, don't be alarmed! An interesting theory supported by some in this business is that a ghostly apparition is genuine if, when you press very gently on one eyeball, you see a double image for a split second. If what you are seeing is a hallucination – a product of the mind – apparently you will only see a single image.

If you have a **medium** in your party it is fascinating to record his or her verdict on contacts made during the séance. Afterwards you can check the medium's connections and findings against established historical fact.

My view is that you cannot get closer to history than actually seeing a ghost. Parapsychologists take a different angle. They prefer in the first instance to talk to people who claim to have witnessed paranormal activity rather than attempting to experience the phenomenon themselves.

Whichever approach you choose to take, be as methodical and unemotional as possible. Your body needs to listen and work in a new way, so try to rest as much as possible in the hours before the investigation takes place. You will probably be up all night, so you will need all the energy and awareness you can muster. Don't confuse your body either by treating it to large doses of alcohol or a large spicy dinner before a vigil; eat sensibly and take along snacks that will give a kick to your blood-sugar levels during the night. Remember at around three o'clock in the morning the body goes into a different mode. This is the time when most people die and most people are born, and it is also the stage during all-night vigils that you need to give your body some fuel. Be as healthy as possible in body and spirit and be aware that even something as simple as a common cold can potentially confuse an investigation. Was that the ghostly tolling of a distant bell you just heard, or a buzz in your ears brought about because you blew your nose?

Many people like to take a **psychic** or medium on a ghost hunt. Do *not* tell them where you are going. Drive them to the location yourself, giving nothing away. You then need to measure exactly how accurate the psychic is. This can be done by creating a map of the location and recording the findings of more than one psychic at each point on the map. Alternatively draw up a list of emotive words, such as 'Happy', 'Angry', 'Murder', 'Child', 'Mediaeval' and so on… and ask each psychic to ring the words they feel most appropriate to particular areas of the location. If you discover that more than one psychic logs the same emotions in the same areas, then you are accumulating useful evidence of a haunting.

I believe the vast majority of psychics have an innate ability to see something the rest of us can't detect. It's a gift in the same way as someone who has the God-given talent to play a piano without music. I also know there are some complete charlatans practising as psychics, but I believe in ghosts and I believe in the supernatural, so I have to believe in mediums.

I have a party-piece when visiting, in particular, ancient sites such as castles, which demonstrates powerfully to me the energy that emanates from stone. I have a crystal on a string that I carry around with me and I have shown tens of thousands of people on my ghost walks how an ancient stone's energy can make the crystal swing on the string of its own accord. All I do is hold the piece of string with the crystal attached in one hand, and place the palm of my other hand on the stone. Within seconds the crystal will start to move – without any assistance from me – and I can only explain this as the energy transferring itself through my body, using the power of the mind. The moment I lift my hand from the stone, the crystal's gyrating action slows down and eventually stops. I don't cheat; I don't have to, and I defy anybody to come up with an explanation for this feat that doesn't have a supernatural foundation.

Before you read on, remember that most people who see ghosts aren't frightened when they see them, because the ghosts usually look like real people. The other important thing to remember is that eight out of 10 ghost stories can be accounted for; it's the other two you need to worry about!

So sleep well, and don't have nightmares.

GLOSSARY OF GHOSTLY TERMINOLOGY

Amulet is an item that has the power to stave off ghosts and evil spirits.

Angel is something often mistaken for a ghost, but in fact is a holy and protective messenger shielding us from harm.

Animal ghosts are believed to be the spirits of animals who survive the death process. Many experts in the paranormal acknowledge the existence of animal ghosts and some investigators even believe animals have what is known as a 'collective soul'. This theory supposes that as many as half a dozen animals at one time may share just one soul.

Apparitions are recorded in the earliest pages of history. This mysterious image of a disembodied spirit can be recognised as a human or animal. They are the most rare type of ghost to capture on film. Ghostly human forms are the easiest to fake, especially with the advanced technology of computers. This makes our job even more difficult, as it is almost impossible to prove the existence of apparitions when using photographs. Ghostly apparitions of ships, trains, cars and other inanimate objects have been seen. Some are said to appear to warn of a disaster that is about to happen, while others are thought to guard sacred places. Some apparitions are not seen, they are heard, or felt.

Apport happens when a solid object appears from nowhere, with the assistance of the spirit in the company of a medium.

Astral body is the energy that separates itself from the human form but still maintains the personality and feelings of the individual. Sometimes others will see them during an out-of-body experience (OBE) or a near-death experience (NDE).

Astral plane can be described as a level of awareness in the celestial world with its own standards and occupants.

Atmospheric apparition is a visual imprint of a person that has died left to be replayed on the atmosphere.

Aura is an energy field that surrounds all living things.

Automatic writing occurs when a ghost or spirit takes control of the writer's hand and pens a message.

Banshee is a spirit that appears before a person's death to howl a mourning song and to welcome them into the afterlife. It is also Ireland's most famous ghost. The correct pronunciation of this female spirit's name is 'bean si' and she is said to associate herself with Irish families – particularly if their surname starts with the letter 'O' – and she is more likely to be seen by a third daughter. Her appearance is said to be the portent of death for a family member, announced by crying and wailing during the hours of darkness. The sound is said to be like that of two cats fighting, only much worse. The tragic relative might be thousands of miles away in another country, and the wailing can apparently be heard for several nights in succession until the actual death occurs. The woman herself appears in contrasting ways. Sometimes she is described as a strange-smelling small, ugly hag dressed in rags. At other times she appears as a young and beautiful woman in a green dress, her eyes red and swollen from constant crying. A third type of banshee has also been reported, but it is not clear whether she is young or old, as she has no clear features, with holes where her eyes should be. The common factor linking all three types is very long hair that streams out in the wind. Folklore dictates that when a banshee is disturbed by a mortal person she will not appear again while that generation lives, but will return to haunt future generations.

Bi-location describes the phenomenon where someone can be in two places at the same time.

Birds were at one time believed to be messengers of the dead – when one tapped on a window, it was said to signify that a ghost was looking for another spirit to join it. Certain birds, such as sparrows, larks and storks, were said to transport to earth the souls of people from the Guff, or 'Hall of Souls', in heaven. Other birds, especially crows, were believed to carry the spirits of humans onto the next plane of existence.

Boggart is a word used chiefly in the north of England to describe a particularly nasty type of ghost. Boggarts are said to enjoy crawling into victims' bedrooms at night and pulling the bedclothes off, slapping, pinching and biting people, especially on the feet. In appearance they are said to be truly frightening, with sharp, long and yellowing teeth.

Bogies, like the Irish banshee, are said to make a wailing noise. An unpleasant spirit with a preference for haunting children, the bogie, according to British folklore, is foul-smelling, black, short and hairy with an ugly, grinning face. Perhaps it belongs more to the language of parents, hence the warning: 'Don't be naughty, or the bogie man will get you!' Bogies were once thought to be the most powerful of ghosts, having apparently once served the Devil by doing evil deeds against mankind.

Cats, next to dogs, are the most common form of animal spirits. The ghost cat is believed to have its spooky origin in ancient Egypt where cats were often worshipped, especially at Bubastis, where many thousands of mummified cats have been excavated. Historically the Devil was believed to be able to take the form of a cat, and cats were often thought to be witches' familiars.

Cemetery lights hover over graves after dark as bluish balls of light.

Channelling is a form of spirit possession that occurs with a medium who is communicating with an unseen entity to gain wisdom or gain knowledge of future events.

Clairaudience, a skill claimed by many mediums, is when someone has the ability to hear the voices of ghosts and other sounds that are inaudible to the human ear. These disembodied voices of the dead, or other entities, normally tell of events yet to happen. Many mediums say that they can hear dead relatives passing on information from a place they call 'the Spirit World'.

Clairvoyance is being capable of seeing events in the future or past through the mind's eye. In its simplest form, clairvoyance is to 'see with sight beyond the normal human range of sight'. A clairvoyant can see visions of events that have already happened, are actually happening or are yet to happen.

Clairsentience is, some believe, a basic human instinct finely attuned and polished. If you are clairsentient, you have the ability to feel and know things that have been, are, and are yet to be.

Cold reading is done when a psychic has no prior knowledge of the sitter.

Cold spot is an area in a haunted place where the temperature drops by several degrees. Temperature can also rise in heat by several degrees, indicating the presence of a fire in the past.

Collective apparition occurs when more than one living person sees a ghost or spirit simultaneously.

Collective unconscious is a term to describe a form of analytical psychology developed by Carl Jung. It represents the collective memory of all humanity's past and is held somewhere inside the unconscious mind.

Conjure is an act to summon a spirit to manifest itself for a desired task or to answer questions.

Corpse candle is a term referring to balls of firelight that can be seen to dance above the ground.

Crisis apparition is the vision of someone that will appear during waking hours or in a dream at the moment of a crisis.

Crossroad ghosts have been reported for centuries, and no-one knows quite why. Some researchers maintain that crossroads are more likely to be haunted because of the number of suicide victims buried there. The superstition behind interring the dead at such places lies in the Christian belief that the cross is a form of protection from demons, vampires and other supernatural night creatures. This theory, however, is thrown into doubt when it is considered that excavated human remains pre-dating Christianity have been unearthed near crossroads all over the world.

Deathwatch is a strange turn of phrase connected with a species of beetle known as the deathwatch beetle, which taps on wood. Many believe the beetle can sense the approach of death and taps in acknowledgement of spirits arriving to take the soul to its next destination.

Dogs have been reported in ghost form all over the British Isles. These spectral dogs are said to vary in size and some have been described as small but with extremely large eyes. They can also be white, black, vicious or gentle. The

Lancastrians have a ghost dog known as a Striker; in Wales there is the Gwyllgi, while Derbyshire boasts Rach Hounds and Gabriel's Ghost Hounds.

Doppelganger is a German word to describe a ghost that is the double of a living person. Those who experience seeing their double are said to be heading towards misfortune in the near future. Confusingly, other investigators are adamant that the doppelganger is also an indication of good fortune, though recorded incidences of them being a good omen are rare. People associated with the haunted individual are also reported as having seen the doppelganger at a place where the living counterpart was nowhere near.

Dowsing is the skill of seeking answers and interpreting them through the use of rods or a pendulum. Dowsing is widely used as a simple but effective way of searching for such things as lost coins, water and ghosts. It is also used to conduct geophysical surveys.

Drudes are mature witches or wizards, and reports of this nightmare ghost date from ancient England. The drude is said to be well versed in the art of magic and able to cause a ghost to appear in the dreams and nightmares of their chosen victims.

Duppy is the name given to a well-known West Indian ghost said to be able to walk the earth only between the hours of dusk and cock-crow. The duppy can be summoned from its grave by an act of ceremonial magic to do the bidding of a witch. The ceremony involves mixing blood and rum together with other substances. This concoction is then thrown on the grave of one known to have been an evil person when alive, as the duppy is widely believed to be the personification of evil in a human.

Earthlights are balls of lights or variable patches of lights appearing randomly and with no explanation as to what causes them.

Ectoplasm is a strange substance said to extrude from the sweat glands, mouth, nostrils and genitals of some mediums while in a trance-like state. A solid or vaporous substance, it is produced by a medium during a trance to reach a dead person. Ectoplasm, or teleplasm, is derived from the Greek words *ektos* and *plasma*, meaning exteriorised substance. There are researchers who claim that the substance is similar to pale white tissue paper, cheesecloth, or fine silk strands that all gather together to make a human shape. Others say the substance is like human and animal tissue. Most reports of ectoplasm have been revealed to be hoaxes. Some mediums have gone to the lengths of taking cheesecloth and rigging it to drop from a part of the body (the nose, mouth or ears). Some mediums even swallowed the cheesecloth and then regurgitated it later during the séance.

Ectoplasmic mist will usually show up in a photo as a misty white cloud to indicate the presence of a spirit. The mist is not seen when the picture is taken. These mists can vary in colour from grey and black to red and even green.

Elemental spirit is a rather curious type of ghost said to be a spirit that has never existed in human form. For this reason, occultists insist they are ancient spirits representing Earth, Air, Fire and Water that predate man. Elemental spirits are often associated with haunted stretches of woodland and rivers, mountains and valleys.

Elves are spirits of nature. Spiteful creatures, they are suffering as lost souls trapped between two worlds; not evil enough to go to hell; not quite good enough to be accepted into heaven.

EMF (Electro-Magnetic Field) meter is a device that can pick up electronic and magnetic fields. It can also detect any distortions in the normal electro-magnetic field.

Entity is a term that refers to an intelligent being who is no longer inside their physical body. They have the power to provide information to all individuals who are sensitive to their vibrations.

ESP (Extra Sensory Perception) represents an ability to gather information beyond the five human senses.

EVP (Electrical Voice Phenomenon or Electrical Visual Phenomenon) is a method by which a spirit's voice is detected by means of a recording device. It is also possible to pick up visual images of a known dead person on computer and TV screens, even when they are not switched on.

Exorcism is a religious ceremony where an attempt is made to expel a spirit that may have taken up residence inside a house or a human being. The ceremony usually involves a clergyman such as a priest, often specially trained, who will say prayers and repeat loud exhortations, often burning candles and sprinkling holy water while incense is burned. Exorcism is actually a modern version of the old Christian practice of excommunication – the rite of 'Bell, Book and Candle' – where sinners were eliminated from further entering the faith by a priest who would ring a small bell and slam the Holy Bible shut, often after reading the Malediction. The priest would then extinguish the burning candles. Modern mediums claim to be able to conduct exorcisms without the usual religious trappings by psychically contacting the spirit causing the problems and convincing it to move on to the next spiritual plane of existence. In some cases it is believed that ghosts in need of an exorcism are spirits that have not come to terms with their passing, especially where their demise has been untimely or tragic.

Exorcist is an individual – usually a religious holy man – who is skilled in removing demons from within people or locations.

Extras is a word used to describe faces or whole images of people that mysteriously appear on photographs. There are many reported instances of pictures revealing the image of a long-dead relative, or even someone still alive but living thousands of miles away, when they are developed. In the early days of photography, many of these wispy images were faked, but there are a small number of examples that defy explanation even today.

Fairies are tiny, invisible mythical beings. The pranks they play are sometimes mistaken for the activities of ghosts or poltergeists. Many types of fairies are believed to exist with each one being connected to an element, as in earth (Gnomes), fire (Salamanders), air (Sylphs), and water (Undines), and the colour green is apparently sacred to them. They are said to live in hills, valleys, among the trees and also where there are ancient burial mounds and ancient stone circles.

Family apparition is a ghost that haunts one particular family. When the ghost appears it is an omen that someone in the family is going to die.

Fireball is a Scottish phenomenon. Described as a medium to large sphere, it moves in a smooth and often slow way, most often over stretches of water. Fireballs are thought to be the souls of the departed returning to earth to guide the souls of people who have recently died to the next world.

Galley beggar is an old English ghost referred to as early as 1584 in Reginald Scot's work, *The Discovery of Witchcraft*. This ghost has the appearance of a skeleton and its name is derived from the word 'galley', meaning to frighten or terrify. The classic image is that of a screaming skeleton – head tucked under one arm – encountered on a country road.

Ghosts are different forms of apparitions of deceased human spirits that can appear to any of our five senses. They can be seen as a shadowy human or animal form. They can be heard and may even emit a familiar or offensive odour. They are trapped between worlds.

Ghost buster is a specialist in clearing an area of ghosts, poltergeists, spirits or other haunted activity.

Ghost catcher is a type of wind chime that will clink together as a ghost wisps by.

Ghost hunt describes a conscious effort to search out a known ghost or to visit other places suspected to be haunted.

Ghost-hunter is a person who seeks to find ghosts or haunted places and tries to determine what type of spirit activity is taking place, and why.

Ghost investigation involves going into an area looking for ghosts or hauntings under controlled conditions. Reports are made to document the events. Listing all the reading of the equipment along with time, weather, and temperature as the project unfolds becomes valuable information for the research.

Ghoul is a grotesque, evil spirit with a terrifying face that gains its sustenance by robbing a grave to eat the flesh of the recently deceased. The ghoul was at one time the common word for a ghost in Arabia.

Graveyard ghost is a ghost believed to have special abilities. According to folklore, the first person to be buried in a churchyard was believed to return to guard the site against the Devil. Because this task was so great, a cat or dog was often buried before any human, so it would become the guardian of the dead and remain so until the Crack of Doom.

Gremlins are a recent phenomenon, originating from World War Two in 1939–45 when pilots flying dangerous missions reported seeing strange goblin-like creatures in the aircraft with them. A 'gremlin in the works' is common parlance now for when machinery grinds to a halt.

Grey lady is said to originate from Tudor times. Some say it refers to the ghost of a woman who has been murdered by her lover or one who waits for the return of a loved one. There's another theory that these ghosts represent the Dissolution of the Monasteries, which resulted in the death of many monks and nuns, who would have been dressed in grey habits.

Hallowe'en can be traced back long before the advent of Christianity. Our ancient pagan ancestors celebrated the 'Feast of the Dead' by lighting great bonfires across the country to summon the dead and placate them by offering burnt sacrifices. The Christian Church is thought to have moved the bonfire tradition to 5 November, marking Guy Fawkes's fate, in an attempt to dilute the true meaning of the night. Modern witches still celebrate the night of 31 October by holding feasts and performing magic rituals. According to legend, Satan opens the gates of hell at the stroke of midnight and all spirits of evil are set free to wreak havoc on earth. By cock-crow these spirits must return to hell, where the gates are slammed shut at the first sight of dawn. Any spirit left outside would disintegrate forever.

Haunted chair is an essentially English phenomenon refer-ring to people who have a fondness for a particular armchair coming back as a ghost and being seen in the same chair.

Haunt is the place where the ghost or spirit continues to return. Ghosts usually haunt places and not people.

Haunting is used to describe the repeated display of paranormal activity in a particular area. Some hauntings are thought to be poltergeist energy from a disembodied entity trapped in a certain location or by the energy left behind from a very strong tragic event or accident. Occasionally, hauntings appear to be an intelligent ghost trying to make a connection with someone on the earthly plane to give a message. People can also be haunted, as can any item that may have belonged to someone deceased.

Headless ghosts are the spirits of people whose death occurred because they were beheaded. There is also evidence to suggest that these types of apparitions may be connected to the ancient practice of beheading the corpses of people suspected of being connected in life with witchcraft and sorcery.

Headless horsemen in ghost tradition are believed to be the results of riders who may have been ambushed and decapitated while riding at speed through wooded glades. Another theory is that headless riders are ancient chieftains who lost their heads in battle and still wander the earth in search of their dismembered heads.

Iron is believed to be a sure antidote against all kinds of bad magic and evil spirits.

Lemures is the Roman word given to evil ghosts who return to haunt relatives and friends. Ceremonies to placate these spirits were often held in ancient Rome.

Ley lines are the invisible lines that run between sacred objects or locations.

Luminous body is the faint glow in a dead body to signify a soul's impending departure.

Malevolent entities are angry spirits, often seeking revenge. They sometimes attach themselves to a living being, causing them discomfort and distress. They tend to impose their anger or depressed personality on the human being they possess.

Materialisation is the ability claimed by some mediums to bring into vision a spirit or ghost. One of the first recorded incidents occurred in America in 1860 and was performed by the Fox sisters, founders of modern day spiritualism.

Medium is someone who can communicate with the dead. During a trance state the medium allows the spirit to take over their body so they can deliver a message to the living. The medium does not remember any of this once they come out of the trance. Today the new mediums refer to this as channelling. The big difference is that nowadays the medium remains completely conscious of what he/she says and experiences through the spirit.

NDE (near-death experience) is when a person dies and is revived after a short period of time. The person remembers their death experience and can recall visions of the afterlife, which include ghosts and other paranormal events. Survivors of this experience say it changes their whole outlook on death and they feel as if they can live better lives after this realisation.

Necromancer is a person considered to be a sorcerer or wizard, who has the power to raise the dead and force the spirits to obtain information about the future.

Orbs are globe-shaped lights of energy caught on film, usually during a haunting or other paranormal experience. Orbs are believed to represent the spirit of an individual that has died. They are made up of the energy force that powered their body in life. They may vary in size, colour and density.

Omen is a prediction of a future event.

Oracle is a prophet that can communicate with spirits, ghosts and gods to obtain information.

Ouija Board is a board with cards of numbers – zero to nine – the letters of the alphabet, and the words 'yes', 'no' and 'goodbye' printed on the surface. A glass beaker or wine glass is placed on the table and the consultation can then begin. The board comes with a planchette (a pointer) and once you lightly place your hand on it the pointer will spell out the answers to the questions asked by the players. This 'game' can be dangerous if participants are not fully aware of what they are doing and are not educated in psychic science.

Paranormal is any experience that happens beyond the range of scientific explanation or normal human capabilities, including hauntings, telekinesis, telepathy, clairvoyance, or any other rarity that cannot be justified by the five senses.

Perfumed ghosts manifest themselves in the form of a scent. Many people have experienced smelling the favourite scent of a deceased relative, such as an aunt or grandmother.

Phantom coaches are also known as 'death's messenger', and are apparently seen in silent progress before a death in the family. The horses are always said to be headless and the coaches are described as black and sometimes have the appearance of a hearse. The skeleton-like driver is usually viewed as horrendously ugly, with a fixed grin.

Planchette is a pointer used with an ouija board to communicate with spirits, ghosts, or entities of a higher plane.

Poltergeist is a noisy and sometimes violent spirit. While ghosts haunt and like solitude, poltergeists infest locations and prefer company. The name 'poltergeist' means 'noisy ghost'. Known traits of the poltergeist are banging, thumping, moving objects, levitating, and causing fires. These same results can also be attributed to an unconscious outburst of psychokinesis. More researchers of today feel that much reported poltergeist activity is related to psycho-kinesis rather than a ghost.

Possession is when an evil entity takes over a human body and forces the soul out. This allows the spirit to use the host by exerting its own will. This may totally adjust the host's current personality. Women aged under 20 are most commonly attacked in this way and show clear signs of emotional distress. The discarnate spirit seeks out humans to display emotions of anger, revenge and resentment.

Precognition is the foreknowledge of future events.

Psychic is a person who tunes into phenomena beyond their five senses and has the ability to see or sense the future, present and past. The talents of a psychic include but are not limited to hearing voices, seeing spirits and knowing what might be happening in the future. Unfortunately these gifts have been misinterpreted as mental illness for some. Psychics have also been referred to as seers or sensitives.

Psychokinesis is the ability to move objects using only the power of the mind.

Psychomancy is the ancient art of reading future events through the appearance of ghosts, interpreting what their manifestations to the living might mean.

Purgatory is the place where the souls of the dead must go to be cleansed of all their sins before being allowed into heaven, according to Catholicism.

Reciprocal apparition is an experience where the individual and ghost see and react to one another.

Reincarnation is the belief that once a person dies their soul returns to a new body where it will continue to learn lessons about life and how to reach enlightenment. Many reincarnations may be necessary for the soul to learn and become closer to the goal of perfection.

Retrocognition is the foreknowledge of past events.

Salt, according to ancient customs, is an antidote to all manner of witchcraft and evil spirits. It is said anyone carrying salt in his or her pocket is protected, even against the Devil himself. Placing salt in every corner of rooms in a haunted building is also said to subdue wicked spirits.

Scrying is a form of divination in which an individual stares deeply into an object such as a crystal ball, mirror or flame, in order to see an image that might appear. Such images – usually generated by a spirit – can be symbolic and give answers to a question.

Séance consists of a group of people sitting in a circle holding hands in the hope of contacting the dead. The procedure is conducted by a medium that goes into a trance, as a vehicle for the deceased spirit to take over and communicate with loved ones, sometimes through a spirit guide. Knocking or rapping sounds can also be heard during a séance. The word is of French origin, meaning 'a sitting', and there's no limit to the number of participants, though even numbers apparently get better results.

Sensitive refers to a person who can detect paranormal events beyond the range of their five senses.

Shaman is a medicine man or witch doctor who can communicate with the spirits during a trance and who also possesses the power of healing.

Sixth sense is to have the power of perception in addition to the five senses. It is also a popular term for ESP.

Smudging is a form of cleansing or clearing a spirit from an area by using incense to purify the area.

Spectre is most commonly used now to describe a ghost that is faked or the result of natural factors.

Spirit guide is a heavenly spirit or guardian angel that is present and offers help to the individual to which it is attached. This help may be a simple feeling that comes over the person when they need guidance for a problem or situation. Some people claim they can communicate with their guides at all times.

Spirit photography is usually a photo that contains a face or form believed to be that of a deceased person.

Spiritualism is a belief structure that assumes that spirits and ghosts can communicate with the living.

Supernatural is when an unexplained occurrence take place out of the realm of the known forces of nature. The experience usually involves spirits.

Table-tipping (typology) is a type of communication with the spirit world by using a table. Participants start out with any size table and surround it with a number of people. Everyone places all five fingers lightly on the table. All together the group chants, 'Table up, Table up'. Usually the table will start to quiver or lift to one side. If someone in the group has strong energy the table might rock back and forth or lift off the floor. At this point a question may be asked with a response from the table tapping, once for 'yes' and two for 'no'. If there is a non-believer present the table will probably not move. This type of entertainment can be dangerous and is not recommended to those not skilled in psychic science.

Talisman is a protective charm or amulet said to have the ability to ward off evil.

Telekinesis is where a person can move an object through the power of thought without physical means to move the object.

Telepathy is a method of communication from mind to mind, sometimes across great distances.

Teleportation happens when an object is transported from one location to another by disappearing and then reappearing in a different place.

Time slips occur when the past and present collide at a location.

Trance, a state between being asleep and awake, is where a medium uses his or her body as a channel for waiting spirits to pass messages through to living relatives and friends.

Transmigration is the belief that a soul can move from body to body through the process of reincarnation.

Vassage is a spirit that inhabits a scrying crystal. During a scrying session, the spirit communicates by forming literal or symbolic images.

Vengeful spirits return from the dead to avenge terrible wrongs that have been done to them.

Vortex is a small tornado-shaped image that shows up on pictures when there is a spirit present. Orbs can apparently be seen rotating inside the shaft. Sometimes the vortex is so dense it will cast a shadow. It is believed that the vortex is a means of travel for spirits in the orb form.

Wakes are a noisy ancient custom of watching over the dead while vast amounts of alcohol are consumed. This tradition, especially popular in Ireland, is based on the theory that drinking – as alcohol is a cleanser – helps the spirit of the deceased on its journey to the next world. Music, singing and laughter are encouraged, as it is believed loud noises keep evil spirits at bay.

Warlock is often used to describe a male witch, but this is insulting to many so-called warlocks, as the word has been used in the past to describe a traitor.

White ladies have been seen all over the British Isles, traditionally haunting castles, mansions, halls and even bridges and stretches of water. In ancient times, pagans, to give them a safe passage, apparently sacrificed young women to river gods.

Will-o'-the-Wisp – also known as jack-o-lantern, ignis fatuus, corpse candle and foolish fire – is a ball of flame that floats in mid-air. Such phenomena have also been observed bobbing or dancing just above the ground in yellow and blue flames. These wondrous episodes have been recorded since Roman times. The Native Americans believe them to be a fire spirit warning everyone of danger. The Germans thought the balls of flame were lost or trapped souls that couldn't move on. In Africa some believed that the Will-o'-the-Wisps were witches trying to scare sinners into behaving properly. In Russia, these lights represent the souls of stillborn infants. Throughout Europe when these lights appeared it was thought to be evil spirits that couldn't enter heaven but were not evil enough to be condemned to hell. It would be foolish to follow these strange dancing lights.

Witch is a person – particularly a woman – who practises witchcraft. Most worship nature, but there are different types. Most modern witches would not use their powers for evil, preferring to help human, animal and spiritual awareness. An unwritten law is that witches cannot reveal to anyone what they are or how they practise their art in the belief that silence is power, and power brings knowledge.

Wizard is someone with remarkable abilities and usually proficient in the art of magic. Most male witches prefer this title.

Wraiths are claimed to be the ghost of a person on the edge of death whose appearance should be seen as a warning to the witness that their days are numbered.

PART TWO

THE GHOST
TOUR OF
GREAT BRITAIN

NOTTINGHAMSHIRE

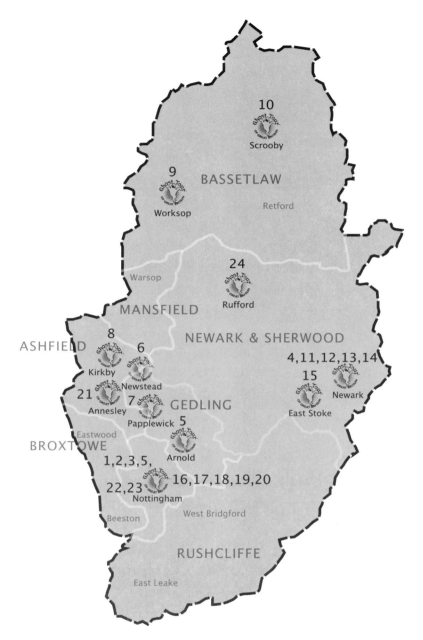

1	Ye Olde Trip to Jerusalem	9	The Devil's Stone, Worksop	17	Rotunda Pub
2	Gallows Hill	10	The murders of William and	18	The Bell Inn, Market Square
3	Bestwood Lodge		Mary Yeden	19	Nottingham Castle
4	RAF Syerston	11	Ossington Coffee Palace	20	Foreman Street
5	Furlong Street, Arnold	12	St Mary Magdalene	21	Annesley Hall
6	Newstead Abbey	13	The White Hart Inn	22	Galleries of Justice
7	The Ghost of Bessie Sheppard,	14	Old Bakery Tea Rooms	23	Colwick Hall
	Papplewick	15	East Stoke Village	24	Rufford Abbey
8	Duke of Wellington, Kirkby	16	The Old Vic, Fletcher Gate		

INTRODUCTION

The East Midlands county of Nottinghamshire boasts great parks, a grand castle, fine houses, a royal heritage and an eclectic landscape featuring the world famous Sherwood Forest. Pre-historic hunter-gatherers lived in this woodland, and in the year 958AD Sherwood was known as 'Sciryuda', meaning 'the woodland belonging to the shire'. It became a royal hunting forest after the Norman invasion of 1066 and was extremely popular with Norman kings such as King John and Edward I.

Nottinghamshire's worldwide appeal, however, is probably more to do with its famous sons than its celebrated landscape, and to many around the globe the word Nottingham is synonymous with just one name: Robin Hood.

It was in Sherwood Forest that this legendary outlaw, fierce enemy of the Sheriff of Nottingham, made his name, probably in the 1200s. By this time the woodland stretched to around 100,000 acres – one fifth of the entire area of Nottinghamshire.

The main London to York road, called 'The Great North Way', ran through Sherwood, and it was here that travellers often found themselves pulled up by robbers living outside the law. Consequently, these criminals became known as 'outlaws'. Whether or not they actually distributed their ill-gotten gains to the poor after stealing from the rich is a matter for debate!

These days, Sherwood Country Park attracts half a million visitors every year and is a heritage site of international significance.

Though his fame has been spread by numerous books and films, Robin Hood is not alone as a famous son of Nottinghamshire.

George Gordon Byron is renowned as one of the world's finest and most famous poets. Byron – later Lord Byron – began writing in 1798 from a house in St James's Street in central Nottingham. His ancestral home, Newstead Abbey, 10 miles north of the city, is the subject of one of the ghost stories in this book, and, as a boy, Byron fell in love with the ghostly halls and spacious grounds of Newstead, which had been presented to the Byron family by King Henry VIII. Money problems, scandal and a failed marriage prompted Byron to quit England in 1816, and he died eight years later, helping Greece to win its independence from Turkish rule. Mourned profoundly by the Greeks, Byron became a hero throughout their land. His body was embalmed and Byron's heart was removed and buried in Missolonghi. His remains were then dispatched to England, where, despite a public clamour, burial at Westminster Abbey was refused and Byron's body was placed in the vault of his ancestors near Newstead. Ironically, 145 years after his death, a memorial to Byron was finally placed on the floor of Westminster Abbey.

D.H. Lawrence, a Nottinghamshire novelist, storywriter, critic, poet and painter, also justifiably can be described as one of the greatest figures in English literature. David Herbert Lawrence was born in 1885 in Eastwood, and his birthplace is now a museum to the writer's memory. The fourth child of a heavy drinking coal miner, Lawrence was educated at Nottingham High School, worked as a clerk in a surgical appliance factory and then for four years as a pupil-teacher. After studies at Nottingham University, Lawrence briefly pursued a teaching career before concentrating on his writing. Much of his work explored deep conflicts in relationships, and Lawrence scandalised the world with his controversial work *Lady Chatterley's Lover*.

Today, Nottingham is a cosmopolitan city with a diversity of cultures. The regional capital of the East Midlands, it has many other claims to fame, not least its fine lace heritage, football, cricket, the Boots Company and Raleigh Industries. The Goose Fair, an annual early October fair, dates back more than 1,000 years and is the largest event of its kind in England.

Although Nottingham gives every appearance of being a modern city and a great place to live, it has a proud history and heritage and many fine old buildings remain, including Georgian town houses, the 15th century Church of St Mary on High Pavement and numerous fascinating old pubs, some with mediaeval origins.

And it was at one of these ancient hostelries in the city of Nottingham that I began my ghost tour of this intriguing county.

I

YE OLDE TRIP TO JERUSALEM

What better place to start my tour of haunted Nottinghamshire than the Ye Olde Trip to Jerusalem, a pub that dates back to 1189AD and is reputedly the oldest in England. A pub this old just has to be haunted!

Carved into the rock and connected with a labyrinth of sandstone caves at the foot of Nottingham Castle, Ye Olde Trip to Jerusalem is a magnate for visitors. Although much of

Photographs of elephant rock and the entrance to Mortimer's Hole, the passage through which a gang entered Nottingham Castle and captured Mortimer after murdering the King.

The lower section of Mortimer's Hole, where cries of mercy from Lady Isabella to her son have been heard.

the inn's history is not well recorded, an archaeological dig in 1974 proved the location of the original castle brew house could only have been that of the caves of Ye Olde Trip to Jerusalem. In all probability, the brewhouse goes back further than the date painted today on the exterior walls of the inn – 1189 – which was the year of ascension to the throne of King Richard I, known as Richard the Lionheart. One of his first acts as King was to crusade against the Saracens who at that time occupied the Holy Land. Legend has it that before fighting this third crusade Richard's knights gathered at Nottingham Castle to rest before journeying to Jerusalem. More particularly, the crusaders stopped off at the inn at the foot of the castle for refreshments – hence the pub's name.

One of the many ghost stories associated with the pub is that of the cursed galleon, which sits strikingly on the top floor of the building in the famous Rock Lounge, accessed via

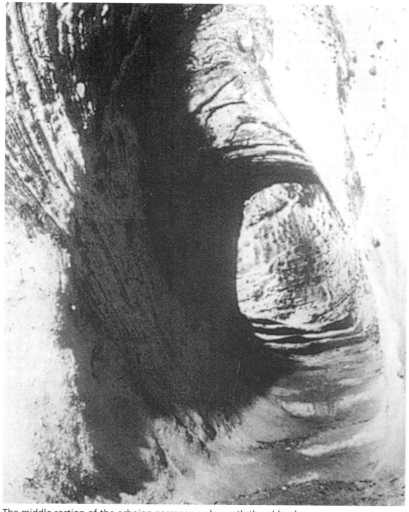

The middle section of the echoing passageway beneath the old pub.

a short stairway. This model of a galleon stands alone, a menacing sight, in a glass case, but what really draws the eye is that the model is absolutely filthy. Its grubby appearance is not through neglect, however, but because of a fascinating and rather morbid story that occurred in the 1930s.

Three workmen were cleaning the galleon and shortly after completing the job the trio died in quick succession under mysterious circumstances. Since that day no one has dared touch the cursed galleon, and consequently the model ship has remained undisturbed, gathering dust. It is kept in a glass case to ensure nobody else can fall foul of its mysterious and dangerous curse.

Adorned with relics from the past, the Rock Lounge also houses the 'pregnancy chair', an ancient wooden chair placed by the fireplace. Legend has it that any woman who sits on it will become pregnant!

There have also been reports of cries emanating from the echoing tunnels and caves beneath the pub. On the night of 19 October 1330 Roger Mortimer, the Earl of March, was seized on the orders of Edward III. Mortimer was the lover of Queen Isabella, who was the widow of Edward II and mother of Edward III, and was occupying Nottingham Castle at the time. The two had plotted and connived to plan the murder of Edward II in 1327 and had ruled the country since his death,

The cursed galleon situated in the pub which remains untouched and gathering dust.

The Cursed Galleon

Roger Mortimer and Lady Isabella, the pair who plotted to kill the King after starting an affair.

the new King having yet to gain his majority. Edward III, his son, ordered the attack, determined to become King and avenge his father's death, and a gang travelled to the inn and were able to enter the castle through one of the secret tunnels below. Edward met them once they were inside the castle and lead them to his mother's room where they met Mortimer and carried him out to a dungeon. He was then taken to London and accused of usurping the king's authority and of the murder of Edward II. He was dragged on a hurdle from the tower and was hanged. The cries that people hear are said to be Lady Isabella, who screamed out to her son to have mercy but to no avail. The passageway in which the gang travelled became known as Mortimer's Hole and is a 105 metre-long tunnel

Numerous other stories are connected with the pub, some of which were explained to me by the current licensee. She described how gas canisters, located in the cellar, often seem to be turned off by unseen hands. The first time this happened, staff presumed the barrels of beer must be empty or the gas had expired. However, on further investigation it was noticed that the gas had in fact been physically turned off. The landlady claimed there was absolutely no explanation for this phenomenon, but as the pub was busy

Photo: S. Lilley

The mysterious galleon encased in glass to ensure no one fall fouls of its curse.

upstairs the strange event had been quickly forgotten. It was only when the gas apparently began turning itself off on a regular basis that the landlady realised something was definitely not right.

This ghostly activity continues to happen roughly once a fortnight and is something the staff at Ye Olde Trip to Jerusalem have simply become used to.

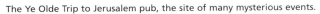

The Ye Olde Trip to Jerusalem pub, the site of many mysterious events.

2

GALLOWS HILL

While in Nottingham, I made my way up Mansfield Road, which leads to the infamous Gallows Hill. It is here that condemned criminals made their final walk to be hanged for their misdemeanours. The journey would start with the individual being taken in a horse-drawn cart or wagon from the County Gaol in Nottingham. They would then be escorted all the way to the top of Gallows Hill to meet their fate.

Traditionally, on the way up the road, the cart or wagon would stop at various pubs and inns, where landlords would send out a complimentary pint of ale or glass of wine. By the time the condemned man or woman reached the gallows, he or she was probably inebriated enough to lessen the full impact and horror of their hanging.

The final pub on the way to the execution point was the Nags Head; after this stop there was no more comforting ale. When the cart eventually reached Gallows Hill, condemned prisoners would usually be told to stand on top of the wagon that had transported them up the hill. The noose would be put in place at the gallows and a prayer would often be offered and hymns sung until the crowd became restless for action. At this point an official would smack the backside of the horse, causing it to draw away, leaving the criminal dangling in the breeze, choking and coughing for anything up to a quarter of an hour until they eventually died of slow asphyxiation.

One famous and tragic story regarding executions at Gallows Hill is that of a gentleman who had been unjustly found guilty of a crime. The man defiantly declined his final drink at the Nags Head and was promptly taken up the hill and hanged at the gallows. Ironically, 10 minutes after his execution, as the crowd began to disperse, a written reprieve for the man was brought to the execution site. Had this innocent man accepted his final drink at the pub, there would have been time enough for the reprieve to be recognised, and he would have lived. It is said even to this day people see the ghost of his tortured figure, which, if you will pardon the pun, tends to hang around the Nags Head longing for the pint that would have saved his life.

An execution site from 1558, Gallows Hill hosted its last hanging – that of William Wells – in 1827. The gallows were removed to Shire Hall four years later. Interestingly, an Act of Parliament passed in 1752 required the bodies of executed murderers to be delivered to surgeons for dissection.

Public executions were so popular in Nottingham that on 8 August 1844 13 people died and more than a hundred were seriously injured in the crush as thousands gathered to witness the hanging in front of the County Hall of one William Saville, a 29-year-old labourer from Arnold who murdered his wife and children with a razor in Colwick Wood.

In a shroud, making his final speech before the cart is driven from beneath him.

3

BESTWOOD LODGE

Bestwood Lodge is a rather secluded place situated grandly among surrounding fields, hills and woods. Yet the lodge is only four miles from the centre of Nottingham and has been in existence in some form for more than 900 years.

Various kings and queens have hunted at Bestwood for hundreds of years, and it was here in 1585 that King Richard III received the news that Henry Tudor, later Henry VII, was heading towards Bosworth Field, the scene of an infamous and bloody battle on 22 August 1485. Richard III was killed in this battle and the crown passed to his bitter opponent Henry.

With so much history surrounding this place, Bestwood Lodge is predictably very haunted. The lodge has so much ghostly activity that on many occasions Jenny Bright, who

Bestwood Lodge, with over 900 years of history captured between its walls.

The Lodge, which used to be a hospital during World War Two, is now haunted by the sounds of dying soldiers. Inside this building is where I heard my first ghost.

runs the famous Nottingham Ghost Walk, has chosen to host her 'Haunted Nottinghamshire Weekends' at the lodge.

I caught up with Bestwood's deputy manager Simon Forbes, who led me to the lodge's most haunted bedroom. Being honest, when I first entered the room there seemed nothing out of the ordinary that might excite the senses, and it certainly didn't look in the least bit haunted.

First appearances can deceive, however, and Simon recounted many strange happenings. Guests using this room regularly sensed they were not alone and reported feeling a strong unearthly presence. Inexplicable physical happenings have also occurred, such as windows, previously locked shut when guests left the room, being wide open on their return. Because of these mysterious goings-on, many of the room's occupants ask to be moved to a more suitable room; others leave the premises altogether.

The lodge itself is extremely special and personal to me as it was here I actually heard a ghost for myself. Twenty-five years ago, while in the Territorial Army as an officer cadet performing the job of radio operator, I was at Bestwood Lodge conducting a training exercise. My platoon had just come under 'attack' and so returned to the ballroom where we were to spend the night. I was the last person to enter the room along with my officer, who went to the bottom of the room while I climbed into my sleeping bag, propping my head against a wall. There were soldiers asleep all around the room, including on both sides of me, and as I settled into my sleeping bag I heard a strange noise coming from the kitchen next door. Anticipating we were about to be attacked again, I went for my rifle, but nothing happened. Suddenly, I heard the sound of a man's voice, a young chap probably around 17 or 18 years of age, and it seemed to emanate from the other side of the wall on which I was resting my head. He was crying and moaning, calling out for a nurse. The noise persisted, and I found myself becoming rather upset and distressed by what I was hearing, to the point where tears were trickling down my face. I became aware I was listening to what sounded like a young man dying. Eventually the haunting voice faded away, and I was able to get to sleep.

A few days after the exercise, I was driving a minibus down to Wales and started up a conversation with a woman from the Royal Army Corps. I told her we had been on an exercise based around Bestwood Lodge, and she informed me she knew the place well and had understood it to be haunted. Indeed, she recalled reading an article in the *Nottingham Evening Post* about the lodge's scary status. I thought back to my experience and was horrified to be told by my companion that Bestwood had been used as a hospital during World War

Two. I am in no doubt that the desperate voice I heard that night was actually a 'recording', somehow retained by the wall on which I was leaning, of a young soldier dying from wounds sustained in battle.

Outside the grounds of Bestwood Lodge in the car park I happened to bump in to Des, a security guard at the lodge. We started talking, and he informed me he had actually seen a ghost in the building. He described to me how one morning, in the recent past, while checking bulbs in the chandeliers of Bestwood's restaurant, he saw the ghostly figure of a man sitting alone at one of the tables. The figure was in his line of sight for only a split second before disappearing, but it was long enough for him to realise what he had seen was no ordinary person. Des described the figure as tall, wearing a long, grey coat and having a Cromwellian-style haircut. He informed me that the same apparition has been witnessed by many other people visiting the lodge.

Des went on to tell me another interesting story about the housekeeper at the lodge who, while on her rounds, thought she saw the bizarre and horrifying sight of a solitary head lying on one of the tanks in the water tower. Alarmed, the housekeeper had immediately tracked down Des, who, on hearing the tale, presumed what his colleague had seen was probably a pigeon. On investigation, however, Des could see nothing out of the ordinary – and the head the housekeeper was convinced that what she had seen on the water tank had disappeared.

4

RAF SYERSTON

Nottingham hosts a multitude of preserved wartime airfields, one of which is RAF Syerston, situated five miles south west of Newark. This was one of a series of new bomber stations built under the second phase of the RAF's 'Expansion Scheme' that occurred in the latter half of the 1930s in response to happenings in Nazi Germany. As World War Two approached, the station was constructed quickly with a mixture of permanent buildings, married quarters and two main hangars.

Opening in 1940, Syerston eventually became the home of 61 Squadron and night bombing operations were launched from here. Later 61 Squadron was joined by 106 Squadron, similarly equipped with Lancaster bombers and commanded by Guy Gibson, who would later lead the celebrated Dambusters Raid.

Regular bombing operations were performed two or three times a week, weather permitting. On one particular October night during the war, a fully loaded Lancaster crash-landed on the airfield and started to burn. Station Commanding Officer Gus Walker dashed into the blaze to try to rescue the crew, but a 4,000lb bomb exploded, the force of which blew him along the runway, severing his arm. Walker lived to become an Air Chief Marshal in the 1960s, his disability never being allowed to interfere with his ability to pilot an aircraft one handed.

Syerston eventually became a training base post-war, until it closed as an operational station in 1976. It is currently home to the RAF's Air Cadets Central Gliding School, responsible for the allocation and maintenance of gliders

This old station is particularly interesting to me because of its old watchtower and the so-called 'Haunted Hangar', both of which still exist in good condition.

Many workers and visitors to the airfield, during and after the war, claimed that they felt an unearthly presence inside this particular hangar. This presence is said to be most obvious during the night when individuals are working alone.

On one such night, not many years ago, the building had been completely locked up securely – there was no way anybody could get inside – yet, inexplicably, the lights in the hangar persisted in turning themselves on and off all throughout the night.

One of Nottinghamshire's airfields, where an unearthly presence has been felt.

Ghostly presences at the hangar also seemed to be detected by police dogs that patrolled RAF Syerston. It is said even these expertly trained animals would cower away from the airfield's haunted places after dark.

During World War Two many young men lost their lives at airfields during training accidents. Certainly, Syerston was used in the early years of the war for so-called 'circuit and bumps' by Oxford training aircraft based at nearby RAF Newton.

Other fliers, as young as 18 and 19, returned, injured, from bombing raids and later died from their wounds. No wonder then that so many airfields remain haunted to this day – these places are inextricably linked with the wretched loss of life of so many young men and women. Perhaps their souls still linger at airfields such as RAF Syerston, troubled because lives so rich in promise were suddenly and tragically cut short.

In close proximity to RAF Syerston is the derelict airfield of RAF Newton. Here is the reported ghost of an airman who is regularly seen wandering aimlessly near homes on the site of the airfield's former runway. Motorists driving along a road that runs parallel to the airfield have been known to pull up to offer the airman a lift, only to discover as they get close to the figure that he disappears from view.

5

FURLONG STREET, ARNOLD

Located in the centre of Arnold in Nottinghamshire is Furlong Street, where rows of terraced houses are situated. It was one particular terraced house on this street, however, that took my interest, as it had been the subject of a considerable amount of poltergeist activity. Many former occupants of the property had reported an incredible amount of strange and inexplicable things happening here, including furniture moving of its own accord and glasses seemingly blowing themselves up. One previous owner of the house explained that the poltergeist activity often became so bad and persistent that on many occasions the family had actually fled the house and slept in their car overnight! The ghostly happenings eventually became so unbearable that the family were forced to sell up and move away.

I was very interested to learn why the poltergeist activity in this particular house was so pronounced, and it didn't take me long to get to the root of the problem. I was told the story of a suicide that took place in the attic of the terraced house. Undoubtedly, the trauma of this suicide somehow generated the energy to prompt the poltergeist activity, which, I am told, still occurs to this day.

FURLONG STREET

6

NEWSTEAD ABBEY

Home of one of Nottinghamshire's most famous sons, Newstead Abbey is also notorious for its many ghosts. In the vast and beautiful gardens at the rear of Newstead is the tomb of Boatswain, the beloved companion of Lord Byron. The inscription on the tomb reads:

'Near this spot are the deposited remains of one who possessed beauty without vanity, strength without insolence, courage without ferocity and all the virtues of man without his vices.'

This praise, understandable perhaps if uttered as a final benediction over human ashes, is but a tribute to the memory of Byron's dog. Boatswain was born in Newfoundland in May 1803 and died at Newstead on 18 November 1808.

Lord Byron himself penned this tribute to man's best friend and is said to have requested that he should be buried in death next to his companion in life. Byron is possibly the most sacrosanct icon of the Romantic Age. The poet's personal beauty, dazzling mind and rash spirit fascinated his contemporaries. Byron was, however, denied his wish to be buried next to Boatswain, and there are numerous accounts from people who report seeing a large dog wandering around the grounds of Newstead Abbey, seemingly searching for its master. When the ghostly animal is approached, however, it simply disappears.

Probably the most famous story associated with Newstead

Abbey is that of a monk who is seen frequently, in the area of the crypt. On one occasion, a workman walking down into the crypt saw a figure he believed to be a monk or a canon, dressed all in black. This ghostly figure appeared in one of the corridors and seemed to the workman to be hovering above the floor. Taking a closer look, he discovered to his horror that the apparition was not only legless – it had no face! As the figure came towards him the workman froze. He could move neither forward nor back as he watched the black monk hovering ever closer to him. As it reached the workman, however, the ghost veered off, disappearing through a wall. Unsurprisingly, as soon as he recovered from the shock, our witness ran as fast as he could away from the crypt and steadfastly refused ever to go down there alone again.

Traditionally, ghost-hunters report seeing the ghostly

The tomb of Boatswain. The dog has been seen haunting the grounds at Newstead.

Near this Spot
are deposited the Remains of one
who possessed Beauty without Vanity,
Strength without Insolence,
Courage without Ferosity,
and all the virtues of Man without his Vices.
This praise, which would be unmeaning Flattery
if inscribed over human Ashes,
is but a just tribute to the Memory of
BOATSWAIN, a *DOG*,
who was born in *Newfoundland* May 1803
and died at *Newstead* Nov.r 18th 1808.

When some proud Son of Man returns to Earth,
Unknown to Glory but upheld by Birth,
The sculptor's art exausts the pomp of woe,
And storied urns record who rests below;
When all is done, upon the Tomb is seen
Not what he was, but what he should have been.
But the poor Dog, in life the firmest friend,
The first to welcome, foremost to defend,
Whose honest heart is still his Masters own,
Who labours, fights, lives, breathes for him alone,
Unhonour'd falls, unnotic'd all his worth,
Deny'd in heaven the Soul he held on earth:
While man, vain insect! hopes to be forgiven,
And claims himself a sole exclusive heaven.
Oh man! thou feeble tenant of an hour,
Debas'd by slavery, or corrupt by power,
Who knows thee well, must quit thee with disgust,
Degraded mass of animated dust!
Thy love is lust, thy friendship all a cheat,
Thy tongue hypocrisy, thy heart deceit,
By nature vile, ennobled but by name,
Each kindred brute might bid thee blush for shame.
Ye! who behold perchance this simple urn,
Pass on, it honours none you wish to mourn,
To mark a friend's remains these stones arise;
I never knew but one — and here he lies.

Who knows what stories lie between the walls of the abbey or why so many hauntings have been reported here.

figures of monks, abbots and canons dressed either in brown or grey, but this man was adamant the figure he saw was wearing clothes that were distinctly black.

His account is interesting because canons who would once have inhabited Newstead Abbey were Augustinians – known as the 'Black Canons' because of the colour of the clothes they wore.

7

THE GHOST OF
BESSIE SHEPPARD

On 7 July 1817 a young girl named Bessie Sheppard was walking alone along what is now the A60 Mansfield Road, making her way from her home in Papplewick in order to find herself a job in Mansfield. What she didn't know was that she was being followed by a dangerous man from Sheffield named Charles Rotherham. He wrongly presumed Bessie had money on her and, knowing she was alone and vulnerable, brutally attacked her by the side of the road, battering her to death with a hedge post. The murderer left the hedge post by Bessie's lifeless body, took whatever he could find of value and ran off.

The 33-year-old man stayed overnight at The Three Crowns Inn, Redhill, where he tried to sell a pair of women's shoes and an umbrella. He left the shoes behind in his room and later sold the umbrella in Bunny. People soon made a connection between Rotherham and the items on Elizabeth Sheppard, and he was tracked down and arrested at Loughborough.

Bessie Sheppard's murderer was taken to Nottingham where he was tried, sentenced and hanged at Gallows Hill for murder on 28 July 1817.

Rotherham's horrific crime united the local community. To ensure Bessie Sheppard was not forgotten, Mr Anthony Buckles and others from Mansfield contributed to a public subscription, erecting a stone memorial in her memory. The stone still stands by the roadside today and reads:

'This stone is erected to the memory of Elizabeth Sheppard of Papplewick who was murdered when passing this spot by Charles Rotherham, July 7th 1817, aged 17 years.'

Not long after the murder took place, reports started coming in from a variety of sources, including coachmen,

The stone memorial for Bessie Sheppard, who was brutally murdered and now haunts the area.

horsemen and people who had been out walking near the spot of the memorial. All claimed they had seen the ghost of Bessie Sheppard hovering around this area. Over time, these sightings became less frequent, eventually ceasing altogether until one day when the stone memorial had to be moved. After this happened, the ghost of Bessie Sheppard began to appear again. Legend has it that every time the stone is moved, usually for road widening work, the ghost of Bessie returns to the spot where she was murdered, no doubt troubled that the stone preserving her memory has been disturbed.

The last known sighting of the ghost occurred in 1956 when a car veered off the road and hit the stone, causing it to move. Shortly afterwards, one dark evening, a young couple driving back to Mansfield from Nottingham looked to their right and saw a white figure dressed in a long flowing dress hovering above the stone. Since that sighting more than half a century ago, no one has reported seeing the ghost of Bessie Sheppard.

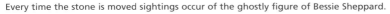
Every time the stone is moved sightings occur of the ghostly figure of Bessie Sheppard.

8

THE DUKE OF WELLINGTON, KIRKBY

I visited one of the oldest pubs in Kirkby in Ashfield, the aptly named Duke of Wellington, which, over the years, has witnessed a great deal of poltergeist activity. In addition to the poltergeist stories, there is a report of an old tunnel that

Poltergeist activity has been reported here for many years by its occupants.

apparently runs from somewhere inside the pub, finishing at the old Church of St Wilfred's.

Inside The Duke of Wellington I met with Vic, a recently appointed landlord of the pub. At the time of my visit Vic had been in charge for only a week but had already witnessed some ghostly goings on. He told me on one night at around 9pm he was serving behind the bar when all of a sudden two of the beer lines stopped working at exactly the same time. Vic went to the cellar to investigate and, to his surprise, found the gas had been switched off. The landlord certainly had not switched the gas off himself and no other member of staff had been down to the cellar. Vic simply could not explain what had happened.

Poltergeist activity is rife in the pub. On frequent occasions, various landlords have reported entering the oldest part of the pub in the morning to discover that all the furniture, including tables and chairs, had been moved. Sometimes furniture had been left upturned in the middle of the floor. These inexplicable happenings were not accompanied by noises in the night and there had been no break-in. Indeed, no one has been able to offer a plausible explanation. I can only guess at the reason behind the mysterious energy that clearly runs through the Duke of Wellington pub. Perhaps it is generated by a deceased former landlord, who, for some reason, finds it necessary to protest to some aspect of how his pub is now being run!

9

THE DEVIL'S STONE

Not far from Worksop is the Carlton in Lindrick Church, which, astonishingly, is more than 1,000 years old. This building is steeped in history, and outside its doors is a stone that has been on the same site for twice as long as the ancient church. It was, therefore, unsurprising that I discovered many mysteries and stories connected with this 2,000-year-old stone.

The most sinister aspect of the relic is its name: the Devil's

The devil's stone and Carlton in Lindrick Church, the sight of many mysteries and stories.

Stone. It is believed in times gone by that Pagan sacrifices were carried out on the site of the church using the blood of a virgin maiden. The girl's blood would drip into the stone, which was used as a Pagan altar. Since those Pagan days there have been stories of the ghostly white figure of a girl, apparently seen floating around the stone.

Perhaps because of this, for many years the stone would be taken inside the church at night until one day it appeared outside on the grass with no explanation as to how it had been moved there. Alarmed by this and perhaps weary with the constant moving of the heavy stone, local residents decided to bury the Devil's Stone in the graveyard where, they believed, it would never to be seen again.

The stone remained buried and forgotten until one day a rather inquisitive vicar gathered a group of schoolboys and dug the stone up, placing it where it now lies, in front of the tower of the church.

Since being unearthed, the Devil's Stone seems to have generated numerous sightings of what has been described as a form of ghost or spirit that appears around the stone and also in the church grounds. Some claim that it is the Devil, but nobody really knows.

What many people believe, however, is that whatever evil events have happened around this stone down the years, the Devil certainly had his hand in it.

10

THE MURDERS OF WILLIAM AND MARY YEDEN

In north Nottinghamshire lies the little village of Scrooby, described in the Domesday Book as 'Scrobi', a berewic attached to the Archbishop's manor of 'Sudtone', now Sutton-cum-Lound. Scrooby is famed as the home of William Brewster. He was one of the Pilgrim Fathers who led a puritan migration to Amsterdam in 1608 before eventually settling in Massachusetts, US.

In 1952 a young man returning to his residence in Retford was trying to get a lift back home. On this occasion he was lucky as a passer-by picked him up, eventually dropping him off at a place called Hawk's Nest. From here he made his way in to Scrooby, but as he turned a corner the young man noticed a little white cottage he had never seen before. This cottage had two windows, one of which pointed up the road and the other down the road. Our traveller noticed a little light glimmering in one of the windows and what appeared to be a figure inside. The appearance of the cottage was confusing for this local man. He had never seen it before and surely it could not have been erected in a single day?

He continued to walk, but just after he had passed the mysterious cottage he heard a woman's blood-curdling scream, which seemed to come from inside the cottage. Looking back towards the building, the young man saw the distressed figure of a frantic woman running out the front door and clutching her head. In panic and some pain, she was shouting and moaning. Then the figure dropped to the floor and lay motionless.

Unsure whether he should go back and help or run for his life, the terrified man noticed another figure rush out the house and disappear into the black night.

Frightened witless by the thought that whoever was causing alarm in the cottage would chase him as well, the man ran off into fields at the rear of the property. Because of his disturbed state of mind, without realising where he was running he actually managed to do a full circuit of Scrooby village, eventually ending up back at the white cottage. Or rather, he landed at the spot where he had *seen* the cottage only minutes before. Because now our bemused traveller discovered the cottage was no longer there. The hedgerow by the side of the building was just the same as it had been, but the cottage itself had vanished.

Bewildered, he continued his journey, but walked in the middle of the road in the hope that a motorist would stop and take him away from this place. Eventually a lorry driver took pity on the bedraggled figure, driving him to his home in Retford.

Here, exhausted and still perplexed by what he had seen, the young man went straight to bed, but, predictably, endured a restless night. Through fitful sleep he dreamed of murder, black deeds and also reported that he was haunted by the sound of a creaking cage and chains rattling in the breeze.

His mind still befuddled by his experiences, the man returned the following morning to the village of Scrooby, which, in daylight, seemed altogether more welcoming than it had the previous night. He plucked up enough courage to visit the village churchyard and, after wandering around for a while inspecting gravestones, eventually found a very old worn-down gravestone on which he could just about make out three words. These words were 'WILLIAM', 'MARY' and 'MURDERED'.

More determined than ever to solve the mystery of the disappearing cottage, he visited the Nottinghamshire Records Office and found to his dismay that on 3 July 1790 William and Mary Yeden had been battered to death with a hedge post by a man named John Spencer who was robbing their house. Spencer was caught, taken to Nottingham and hanged on Gallows Hill. After the murderer of William and Mary Yeden was hanged, his body was tarred and hung up 30ft high in a cage and left to rot while crows pecked at his eyes.

After learning this, the man was sure that what he had seen was a ghost house and the ghosts of Mary and William Yeden, attempting to flee in panic from their Scrooby home.

Only the young man himself knows for sure what he actually saw that evening in 1952. I think, for whatever reason, perhaps because the atmosphere was the same as it had been on that fateful night back in 1790, that the Yedens' horrendous murders were replayed that night and witnessed by an innocent passer-by.

11

OSSINGTON COFFEE PALACE

Newark is an historic town, and it was here that King John, the notorious King who was of course the arch enemy of no less than Robin Hood, was supposedly poisoned to death.

I visited a building formerly known as The Ossington Coffee Palace, which happens to be one of the most haunted buildings in Newark. Outside the main entrance is a plaque

One of the most haunted buildings in Newark, where staff have been terrified by strange happenings.

which reads: '*A perfect copy of a 17th Century hostelry erected in 1882 as a temperance hotel by Viscountess Ossington, a daughter of the fourth Duke of Portland and widow of the First Viscount of Ossington, one time Speaker of the House of Commons.*'

Viscountess Ossington established the place as a temperance house and there were no reports of ghosts or hauntings until after the original 99-year lease expired. At this time the establishment was granted a licence to sell liquor and ever since that day many ghostly occurrences have taken place inside the building.

Down the years many members of staff have been terrified by strange happenings, not least upstairs, formerly the restaurant and the place where most sightings have been made. Here, napkins get thrown around and have been seen floating across the room. Glasses somehow turn themselves over and have even been known to blow up. On one occasion a waitress went up to the room to find all the chairs had been

The plaque on the main entrance to the former Ossington Coffee Palace.

moved from their usual setting around a table and placed in a circle in another part of the room. This was not simply a practical joke played by a member of staff – there was truly no logic to what had happened.

Ossington Coffee Palace still retains a reputation as being very haunted, though the current owners assure me that ghostly activity has calmed down of late. The only slightly unusual happenings today are reports of the rustling sound of a woman's dress and the strong smell of sandalwood. Perhaps Viscountess Ossington is still keeping an eye on the building she once looked after, making sure it is running to the same high standards that she once set.

After learning about the fascinating stories connected with this building, I was lucky enough to bump into a man who was able to give me first-hand accounts of ghostly goings on at the Ossington Coffee Palace. He recalled an event just one year previously, when his son was entertaining guests at his 21st birthday party in the upstairs restaurant. Everyone was enjoying a carefree time when, all of a sudden, three wine bottles began moving simultaneously across linen table cloths, sliding across the dining table before smashing onto the floor. This bizarre poltergeist activity happened in front of all the guests, none of whom could believe their eyes!

Shaken, but not wanting to spoil the mood of the celebration, the 21st birthday party guests put the incident down to 'vibrations'. It is patently obvious to everyone in the room, however, that no amount of vibrations could have caused three wine bottles to mysteriously slide off a table without assistance. Why the poltergeist of Ossington Coffee Palace is so opposed to the drinking of wine in the restaurant, we will probably never know.

MAKE HASTE TIME FLIES

12

ST MARY MAGDALENE, NEWARK

I had previously visited St Mary Magdalene Church in Newark during my time in the Territorial Army back in 1979. I had no idea then that the place was haunted, but it was for precisely this reason that I made my way back to this imposing church for a second time while on my ghost tour of Nottinghamshire.

The magnificent mediaeval building has a spire, reputedly

The mediaeval church of St Mary Magdalene, a landmark for miles around.

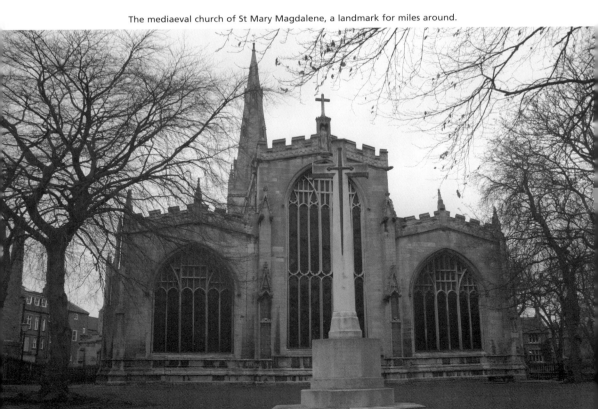

Inside the church in Newark where the ghostly image of a priest has been seen kneeling and praying.

The imposing doorway and decorative internal door of this historic and haunted church.

the fifth tallest parish church spire in the country, which soars to over 230 feet and is a landmark for miles around in the Trent valley. The church can boast structures from four architectural periods, from a crypt dating from around 1180 to two 15th-century chantry chapels of striking quality.

One of the ghost stories associated with the Church of St Mary Magdalene relates to World War Two. During the bombing campaigns of the German Luftwaffe, locals would volunteer to be firewatchers at important buildings, especially those with extensive wooden structures, in order to safeguard them from being burned to the ground.

On one instance two lads who were choirboys at the church were on night watch here at Newark Parish Church. One of the young men went off on patrol and left the other inside the vestry with the door closed. Shortly after the first boy left the vestry, the remaining youngster heard a very loud hammering and battering on the vestry door. Terrified, he stepped away from the door and, as he did so, noticed that the bottom of the door was actually moving with the force of whatever or whoever was banging on the other side. When his friend returned to the vestry, the young choirboy explained what had happened, but was told he must have imagined the whole thing and had obviously been listening to too many ghost stories.

Later that night, however, as the two lads settled down and attempted to get some much needed sleep, the hammering noise started again just as furiously as before, but neither of the startled choirboys dared open the door to see what was behind it. The following morning the church verger came in to check on the boys' night watch and noticed scratches and marks all over the vestry door. The two lads explained at

Photo: D. Redfern

The regimental colour of the Sherwood Foresters.

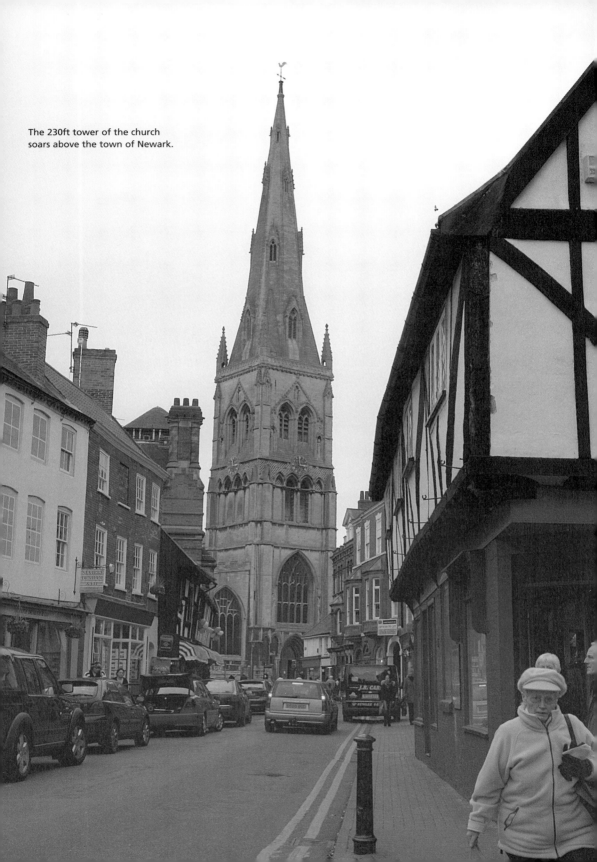

The 230ft tower of the church soars above the town of Newark.

length what had happened during their terrifying watch, but, to this day, nobody knows what really happened in the Church of St Mary Magdalene that night during World War Two.

Another story relates to the same part of the church and involves the figure of a priest who has apparently been seen kneeling and praying here. This is believed to be the ghost of the last Roman Catholic priest at St Mary Magdalene before King Henry VIII took his decisive step against the power of the church in 1538, when he began the Dissolution of the Monasteries.

Perhaps the last Catholic priest of this Newark church is seen regularly re-enacting the last moments before King Henry VIII's soldiers burst into the church, arrested him and took him away to York where he was hung, drawn and quartered for High Treason. Maybe his tormented soul still languishes in his beloved church.

I 3

THE WHITE HART INN, NEWARK

The White Hart Inn in Newark is reputedly the oldest pub in the town – certainly there is a plaque on the wall laying claim to the fact. This mediaeval timber-framed building is also considered to be of national importance, being described by experts as one of the paramount examples of late 15th-century timber-framed architecture in England.

This historic mediaeval inn is the home of poltergeist, said to be the ghost of a man who was executed in the market place.

A paramount example of late 15th-century timber-framed architecture, the White Hart Inn is reputedly the oldest pub in the town.

The pub is home to a poltergeist called George, who is reputedly the ghost of a gentleman hanged outside in the market place before being brought inside the pub to die. In later days, criminals sentenced to death in Newark would almost always be taken to Nottingham to be hanged, but in the early days of rough justice people would be hanged in local market places around the county.

The reason why George would have been brought in to the pub to die is because in those days a condemned prisoner would be made to stand on a cart or wagon while his head was placed in a noose hanging from a scaffold crossbeam. The horse would then be pulled away, resulting in a slow and painful death for the victim. Strangulation would often take up to quarter of an hour.

On some occasions, these wretched people were only half hanged and had to be taken down and moved some place to die. This is probably the reason why the ghost of George haunts the White Hart Inn, as it was in this pub that he drew his last breath.

I met with Martin who works at the White Hart, and he explained to me some of the strange things that have happened during his time at the pub. He told me of occasions when, while the pub was closed, arguments had broken out between staff members. During these arguments coins often flew across the room at the individuals having the argument, a phenomenon that seems to indicate the spirit does not like unrest.

I get the distinct impression that ghostly activity at the White Hart is the result of a poltergeist. Martin went on to tell me there used to be a clock on top of the till, which was often moved by unseen hands. An Australian researcher was so fascinated by George after visiting the pub that he attempted to trace back his ancestry.

Interestingly, these events tend only to occur when there is a bad atmosphere in the pub. Perhaps the negative atmosphere reminds George of the day he was hanged and his excruciating death.

Photo: D. Redfern

The plaque tells how old the pub is and who knows what events have occurred here over the centuries of its existence.

14

THE OLD BAKERY TEA ROOMS, NEWARK

Dating back to the 15th century, the Old Bakery Tea Rooms is situated in the centre of Newark and is known to be haunted.

These tea rooms were not a planned destination on my ghost tour of Nottinghamshire, but when I dropped in for a bite to eat I had an interesting chat with the owner who told me of some of the strange events she has witnessed since she started working here.

She was keen to point out that originally she had been extremely sceptical about the existence of ghosts and entities. However, shortly after buying the building she spent a lot of time in the early morning painting and decorating the premises. One particular morning, at around six o'clock, while working in the kitchen, she heard a little girl's voice calling her name. The voice seemed to come from outside the building. Puzzled, the owner came out from the kitchen to see who was there, but the early morning street was empty; there was no sign of a girl.

The woman thought nothing of this until the exact same thing happened to her again a week later. The same voice – that of a happy little girl – called out to her, but again, when she went outside, there was nobody there.

On another occasion, the woman's husband, who was in

The plaque on the door of the tea rooms where the ghostly voice of a little girl has been heard.

another part of the building, called to his wife asking what it was she wanted. The owner told her husband she had not called him, but he insisted he had heard a woman shout his name, though, on reflection, the voice did seem to be younger than that of his wife.

The little girl continues to haunt this building, a quaint little place in the centre of Newark. It is so steeped in history and well renowned locally that its picture even appears on the front of a Sharps Toffee tin.

15
EAST STOKE VILLAGE

The sleepy little village of East Stoke lies along the old Roman road along the Fosse Way, four miles from Newark, and was once a place associated with death, destruction, battle and the plague.

Mentioned in the Domesday Book, East Stoke is believed to be close to the site of the Roman Ford Ad Pontem, which provided a crossing to Southwell over the River Trent in

The church and churchyard, home of the Weeping Angel of East Stoke a memorial to Julian Barron Ponsforth, who was the 1st Ambassador to the United States of America.

Roman times. The village also lends its name to the Battle of Stoke Fields in 1487 – the last battle of the War of the Roses. This bloody battle saw the defeat of the Yorkists led by Lambert Simnel, pretender to the Earldom of Warwick, by the army of Henry VII, resulting in 7,000 deaths, a large number of them German mercenaries. Many soldiers in the defeated army were cut down as they tried to flee across the river in a meadow that became known as Red Gutter. In the parish churchyard is a memorial to those who died at East Stoke, which reads:

'To commemorate the dead at Stoke Field 16th June 1487. John De La Pole, Earl of Lincoln, Sir Thomas Geraldine, Col Martin Schwartz and 7,000 others English, Irish and German.'

In 1646, when the Great Plague was raging through England, 158 villagers in East Stoke died from the Black Death.

So many people have met their maker at East Stoke, and it

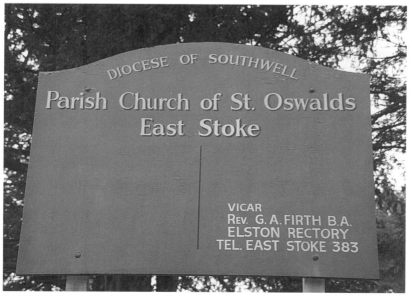

Photo: D. Redfern

East Stoke has been the site of many hideous occurences resulting in many deaths.

is unsurprising that there have been many reports of ghosts haunting the village. Some of the reports mention naked men – not some strange recreation of a stag night in the village, more likely an apparition of Irish soldiers who tended to fight naked with swords and daggers! Many of these reports involve ghosts being sighted on the road known as the Red Gutter because of the vast amount of blood that flowed down the road during the Battle of Stoke Fields.

The churchyard also features a statue known as 'The Weeping Angel of East Stoke', a memorial to Julian Barron Pornsforth who was the 1st Ambassador to the United States of America. Legend has it that the angel weeps real tears of sorrow for all those that have met an untimely death in the village.

One of the many questions I am asked while on my ghost tours is how and why ghosts actually seem to wear clothes! My answer is that the majority of ghost sightings are probably natural 're-cordings' of an event rather than ghosts with the ability to interact. Therefore, we see the ghosts clothed, exactly as they would have appeared in life when their event was cap-tured, almost like a film. This explains why people experience sight-

Photo: D. Redfern

The Weeping Angel of East Stoke, which is said to cry real tears for those who meet an untimely death in the village.

TO COMMEMORATE
THE DEAD AT STOKE FIELD
16TH JUNE 1487.

JOHN DE LA POLE
EARL OF LINCOLN
SIR THOMAS GERALDINE
COL. MARTIN SCHWARTZ
AND 7000 OTHERS
ENGLISH IRISH AND GERMAN

ings of the likes of a coach and four horses, a man with a sword and hat, or a woman in a veil – they are simply watching the equivalent of a video tape that, for some reason, keeps replaying when the atmospherics are right.

Perhaps the village of East Stoke, with its bloody history, also boasts some 'real' ghosts – suffering souls who cannot rest, maybe because they were buried where they were hacked down, in unconsecrated ground.

I talked to a villager who told me of one evening when he was driving with his girlfriend along the road through East Stoke known as the Red Gutter. Suddenly and unexpectedly, his car's engine cut out as they approached a bridge. A White Lady then appeared above them and walked across the bridge before disappearing down a driveway. The couple were struck dumb by what they had witnessed, and as soon as the apparition vanished from view the man restarted the engine with no problems.

This event frightened this villager and his partner so much that he had to give me instructions on how to find the bridge as he refused to take me to the location himself. He has vowed never to return there!

16

THE OLD VIC, FLETCHER GATE

The Old Vic on Fletcher Gate in Nottingham is said to play host to a lady ghost who regularly visits the pub.

Wendy, who has worked at the pub for a number of years, recalled to me how one night she and a colleague were locking up for the day when they glanced down at the CCTV monitors and saw what appeared to be a ghost sitting at one of the tables in the bar. The pair stepped tentatively back into the room for closer inspection, but there was nobody there. Believing it must have been their imagination playing tricks after a long and hectic day at work, they locked up again and took one last look at the monitors. The ghostly apparition had returned, was standing up and actually walking towards the bar as if it wished to be served.

There have been many other incidents involving the pub's CCTV monitors. The figure of a woman wearing an old fashioned Victorian bonnet appeared outside the doorway to the ladies' toilets, seemingly leaning against a wall. Wendy went down to investigate but, just as she feared, by the time she reached the toilets the mysterious lady had vanished.

The same apparition appeared some time later in the same location, apparently sitting on a wooden stool. The manager asked the ghost to leave the pub, and the figure has not returned and has not been seen since.

17

THE ROTUNDA PUB,
NOTTINGHAM

I found it hard to believe when I walked into the bar at the Rotunda pub in Nottingham that this was once a general hospital. With a history of pain, anguish and, of course, death, it is not hard to understand why such a place would be haunted.

Jason Stephenson, licensee at the Rotunda, explained how the sound of footsteps and creaks are often heard in the bar when there is no one else around. This apparently happens on a regular basis, especially late at night.

One specific story Jason related is based on one of the doors inside the pub, which leads away from the bar. Jason was in the cellar one day and his head barman was sitting at the bar with his girlfriend when they both heard a loud bang that seemed to come from behind the door, as if someone or something was slamming it shut. This was promptly accompanied by a puff of smoke, which the bemused barman thought might have been emitted by a smoke machine, used by visiting performers, that was in the room at the time. However, the smoke machine had not been switched on and in any case took several minutes to warm up to the level where it actually churned out stage smoke.

As the pair at the bar continued to look at the door, they were astonished to see what appeared to be the figure of a man walking through the smoke and out into the main bar area. The ghostly figure did not even glance at the barman and his girlfriend, instead choosing to walk the length of the room before disappearing, never to be seen again.

A former general hospital which would have seen much pain, anguish and death over the years.

18

THE BELL INN, MARKET SQUARE

In 1276 the Carmelite monks arrived in Nottingham and obtained lands and property. On what is now Friar Lane, they established a friary and their lands extended to include the site of what is now the Bell Inn, and it is reliably considered that the building was the guesthouse of the friary. The Bell originally served as a refectory of the Carmelite monastery then sited on Beast market Hill, just below St James Street Junction. The cellars of the Bell Inn date from the 12th century and are a combination of natural sandstone and hand-carved caves. It is thought that the Carmelite Friars did the majority of the expansion, and evidence leads to belief that the cave area was used as a kitchen, as there is also evidence of a chimney.

A bonded warehouse is hidden beneath a wooden hatch in the cellar and evidence of the old method of wine sales still exists today, as port cellars and shelves filled with bottles and the steel tracks that housed barrels of wine ready for sale are still clearly display.

In 1539 Henry VIII closed some small monasteries in an effort to tap a valuable source of income. It then became a secular alehouse, taking its name from the Angelus bell, a Latin word meaning 'the noon-day bell', that hung outside the monks' refectory.

The first written evidence of the Bell came about in 1638 when Alderman Sherwin passed away, bequeathing his half of it to the poor, but dendrochronology, dating evidence from timbers in the Bell Inn, gives a date for the building of c.1420.

The Bell Inn has been in the family of current landlord Paul Jackson for 103 years, and during this time there have been many sightings and ghostly activities in this old and atmospheric pub.

On the wall in the restaurant is a large framed photograph of Paul's grandfather, Robert Jackson, who once ran the establishment. Robert Jackson's ghost has been seen by one of the barmaids at the pub walking through the same room in which he appears on the photograph. The barmaid was standing on a ladder cleaning shelves when she felt a strange sensation, as if somebody was behind her. She glanced up just in time to see the apparition disappear through one of the walls.

Photo: S. Lilley

The 12th-century inn where paranormal activity has been reported on many occasions.

Paul's grandfather is not the only family ancestor who apparently continues to visit the pub. Paul also claims to have heard distinct voices he believes to be his grandfather's mother and older brother having an argument in one of the rooms downstairs. This happened one night after closing time when, curious, he went to investigate. By the time he reached the downstairs areas the noises had stopped and everything seemed distinctly normal. Paul went back upstairs and unlocked his office door to do some work and was dismayed to see that the pictures and calendar on a wall were all moving as if someone had just brushed past them. At the same time he also felt something brush against his back and, realising he wasn't alone, made a hasty exit.

On yet another occasion, a deceased member of Paul's family was spotted; a visitor claimed to have seen the figure of a woman Paul later verified as his great grandmother walking through the wall in the ladies' toilets. This made a lot of sense as the kitchens used to be where the figure had been seen, and the visitor described the apparition as seemingly carrying a tray of food. Paul's great grandmother would have spent a lot of her time in the old kitchen. The pub certainly seems to still be home to an abundance of family members who perhaps remain to ensure that the inn they once ran is still being operated properly.

Paul recalled another supernatural event, which occurred in what is now the pub's restaurant. During the middle of the day, two figures in Edwardian-style clothing appeared in a corner of the room during lunchtime service and sat as if they were awaiting a meal before vanishing just as quickly as they appeared. The two characters have been seen a few times in the restaurant, and it is an ongoing joke with the waiters and waitresses that they always disappear before paying the bill!

19

NOTTINGHAM CASTLE

Nottingham Castle, and in particular the famous Long Gallery, have had a fair share of supernatural activities recorded down the years.

The present castle is an eye-catching structure, situated on a sandstone outcrop above the city. It was built by the Whig politician and Prime Minister Pelham-Holles, 1st Duke of Newcastle, in the 18th century. The city later acquired the building and opened here what is thought to be the earliest provincial municipal museum.

One man who knows more than most about the paranormal happenings that go on in the Long Gallery at Nottingham Castle is Pete Barnsdale, an attendant here for more than 32 years. Pete recounted to me some stories he can guarantee are factual, as he personally witnessed them.

One morning in 1995 Pete was just starting his shift and was walking alone along the gallery. It was about 10 o'clock and he was dusting off his jacket as he prepared to meet the paying public and answer any questions about the castle they might have. As he continued his way along the gallery, he heard a famous and familiar noise – the great doors of Nottingham Castle opening.

Because Pete's boss was a stickler for timekeeping and expected the doors to be opened at precisely 10 o'clock, Pete glanced at his watch to check everything was on schedule. As he looked up from his watch, however, he noticed a girl, perhaps aged around 12 and dressed all in blue, was already in the gallery despite the doors being barely open. Pete told me the girl was 40ft away and stood staring at him for about 10 seconds before disappearing as quickly as she had appeared. Confused as to how anyone, especially a child, could have entered the building so quickly, the perplexed attendant ran after her, but, despite checking all rooms along the Long Gallery, could find no sign of the girl dressed in blue.

Frantic to track down the missing child, Pete asked all his colleagues and the man at the castle entrance gate for information, but nobody had seen the girl. Despite being positive that he had seen her, a long and thorough search of the building proved fruitless and there was no evidence to suggest that anyone had been on the premises before 10am.

Three weeks later Pete recalled his encounter to a colleague, who told him on the same day as Pete's curious experience he too had seen the girl in another part of the castle. As Pete's colleague was switching off the lights and locking up the museum for the night, he was surprised to see a girl dressed in blue. The attendant informed the girl she should not be in the museum as it was closing. He asked where her parents were and when the girl did not answer he moved to switch the lights back on, only to find she had vanished.

It seems certain these two castle workers saw the same ghost that day, but she has not been seen here since. Perhaps she was simply passing through, in between two destinations, but we will probably never know the true story.

Another truly terrifying incident occurred in the Long Gallery in 1970 in the early hours one morning at around 2 o'clock. In order to save on electricity costs through the night, the room was only dimly lit, but two security guards who were walking along the gallery with their guard dog were used to this.

However, on this particular night, as the two men entered the gallery as normal, their dog suddenly pulled frantically on its lead and started to bark uncontrollably. The animated dog tugged off its lead and disappeared at speed down one of the corridors. At this point the two men braced themselves, assuming someone was attempting to break in to the castle. Truncheons at the ready, cautiously they began to walk down the famous gallery. What they were to face though was far scarier than any burglar...

Suddenly, from the very far corner of the room, shot a great ball of light about the size of a football. It flew up to the roof, across the walls and continued to bounce all the way down

the gallery. The two men were absolutely stunned to see this brilliant light bouncing from side to side in front of them. The 'ball' created seven or eight arches of flashing light before eventually crashing towards the ground and seemingly exploding on impact.

At this point the gallery became alive with sparks in a scene reminiscent of a fireworks display. In total shock and bewilderment, the two men looked at one another before retreating from the gallery as fast as their legs would carry them. They ran towards the main office and called the police, but by the time officers arrived at the castle all traces of the bizarre phenomenon witnessed by the security guards had gone.

Nobody knows for sure what went on that night in 1970 and certainly no one has since reported seeing the ball of light anywhere in the castle. All that is known is that whatever happened that night it was terrifying enough to cause one of the security guards to go home ill. He could not face being in the building any longer, and a police officer had to stay on with his shaken colleague to keep watch for the remainder of the night.

A 17th-century ducal mansion, built on the site of the former mediaeval castle.

20

FOREMAN STREET, NOTTINGHAM

Situated in the old part of Nottingham near the Theatre Royal is Foreman Street. Towards the end of the 1800s this area of the city had become yet another of Nottingham's long line of infamous red light districts. Consequently, Foreman Street was a fairly popular place around this time.

It was home to a young lady who went by the name of Nellie Banks. Nellie was locally famous around the area and very much in demand, having made a nice little 'career' for herself from the comforts of her home in Foreman Street. Of course Nellie Banks is now long gone, but the house where she once lived still remains, and, as with many of the old houses in Nottingham city, it has been converted into a shop. Until very recently the establishment was called 'Little London Herbal Stores', selling all kinds of herbal remedies, vitamins, food supplements and health products. The gentleman who managed 'Little London Herbal Stores' also owned the entire building in which his shop was situated.

One evening, at around half-past five, the proprietor of the shop went to the front door, locked it and turned the 'open' sign around to 'closed'. Rather than leaving for home, as he would normally have done at this time, he decided to stay behind after hours to get up to date with his accounts. He made himself a coffee, wandered back behind the counter and sat down to begin the laborious task of going through the books. His work continued late into the night until unexpectedly, at around 9 o'clock, his attention was broken by a sudden sound that seemed to emanate from the empty room above. The noise took the form of a very loud, repetitive, slow and monotonously regular banging on the floorboards above the shop's ceiling. He tried to ignore the sound, but it became louder and louder and the banging became faster and faster above him. The noise became so aggressive and vigorous that it began to rattle the light fittings and shake the very contents of the shelves in the shop below.

Understandably frightened and confused, the shopkeeper weighed up his options. He knew it was impossible for anybody to be in the empty room because to get there the person would have had to walk through the shop, up a flight of stairs and through three locked doors. This was scary, but did he have the nerve to investigate? Suddenly, after about three minutes, the noise stopped. Silence descended once again on the Little London Herbal Stores.

A few days later the proprietor was back in the shop doing his day to day business when he got into conversation with one of his regular customers about the strange phenomenon he had experienced. As luck would have it, this customer turned out to be something of a local historian, and he was able to shed light on what had happened that night. He explained how the premises had once belonged to Nellie Banks, who in 1884 was at the height of her prowess, plying her trade with some success from her home in Foreman Street. At the same time a well-respected High Court Judge, an elderly man by the name of Watkins Williams, was on his monthly visit to Nottingham, presiding over some legal cases. After a particularly strenuous day of sentencing, Williams decided to visit Nellie at her home in Foreman Street as a way of letting off steam. The Judge, however, had a weak heart, which unfortunately did not stand up to the evening's activities. It is said he was found dead in Nellie's bedroom later that night – with a curious grin on his face!

Perhaps the noise the shopkeeper heard that night was that of Nellie Banks expertly carrying out the task she did best with Justice Watkins Williams in the final three minutes before his death. This explains the loud and continuous banging sound and the reason it stopped so suddenly!

21

ANNESLEY HALL

I have been back to Annesley Hall on several occasions, to see what is now a sad ruin of what was once an impressive, imposing hall and family home. This beautiful old building would have rung to the sounds of music and laughter up to only 33 years ago, a very proud house, but it is now in a dilapidated state and is an historic ruin after it was severely damaged in a disastrous fire in 1997. Long gone are the deer, the families and the atmosphere of 33 years ago. It is almost unbelievable now. It is still an atmospheric place, even in its current state, but the atmosphere has become colder, more frightening and lonely.

It has a history dating back as far as mediaeval times. It was lived in by the Annesleys, then the Chaworths married in to the Annesley family and then the Musters married in to the Chaworth family. It was also the childhood home of Mary Chaworth, who was the sweetheart of Lord Byron and, as he confessed on his deathbed, his only true love. Legend has it that it was also once the home of Robin Hood and there are numerous reports that tie in with the stories related to the famous legend.

It is believed by a great number of people that Annesley Hall is haunted, some even say it is one of the most haunted buildings in the country. Over the generations, it is hardly

A view of Annesley Hall before the tragic fire that reduced it to ruins.

surprising that there have been many deaths, romances and tragic events that have resulted in the hauntings between its old crumbling walls. There have been many reports of ghost sightings at Annesley Hall, in the rooms and corridors of this eerie place, and many stories of family members and staff that have lived and died in this building that are still in residence.

There are several places in and around Annesley Hall that hide stories and spirits. Here are a few that I know of.

Inside the graveyard at the hall, the most famous grave is that of Commander Chaworth Musters. While on his travels through South America, he met an Indian chief and continued his journey with him for two and a half years. The Indian Chief liked him so much and had enjoyed his company so he made him the King of Patagonia. However, he was not given the usual crown to commemorate the event but a stick was ordered by the chief to be carved instead, which had a human jawbone at the top. The stick is now in the possession of a former worker. Unfortunately the jawbone is missing, but he often feels something outerworldly emanating from the stick that he cannot really explain.

There have been many reports of paranormal activity in the graveyard, which is unusual on consecrated ground. But there have been six witnesses to one ghost, which to me seems conclusive evidence of its existence. A group of people came to the hall one Halloween and as a spooky excursion they walked in to the graveyard at midnight. One of the party cried out as he spotted the ghostly figure of a monk in full habit with the hood up, covering his face. The other members of the party turned and were all witnesses to it, as they stood opened mouthed as he drifted across the ground and faded away in to a mist, as he passed over the fence in the distance. Beyond the fence, further down at the end of an old footpath, is Newstead Abbey, so it would seem that this monk is taking the old route back to the Abbey.

Another sinister and frightening tale was told to me by a member of the hall staff. At the front of the building he had been sitting by the building on the wall underneath with his partner, and he noticed that one of the windows above them was open. He informed a colleague, who went upstairs to try and close it, but he couldn't, the window was stuck fast. He came back downstairs and outside to an almighty bang. The window had slid down and a huge piece of glass landed and was stuck between the legs of the two people sitting below. This potentially fatal experience can be explained away, but it is the firm belief of those involved that this was the act of something from the spirit world because of the ferocity with which it fell and the position in which the dangerous piece of glass had landed, causing no harm to anyone. These beliefs were further added to when, as they were clearing up glass from around the grounds one morning and dumping it in the hall out of harm's way, his partner ran from the building screaming in a real panic. She had heard old-fashioned violin music being played in the hall, which would have often been heard here in times gone by, and also Jack Musters was a very good violinist. Sounds of other music, baths being run and doors slamming have also been heard emanating from the building without any possible explanation, and recently someone even reported the sound of sawing wood coming from a room that was all shut up with no one inside.

Our next ghost story comes from the grounds, down by the lake. This story concerns a well that used to be in the grounds. It was a private well for use by the people in the hall and there was another one further down the road for the villagers. The location of the well is not known as it was covered over with railway sleepers then filled in due to the building of the M1. There was a tale of a farmer's daughter in the area who had gone missing in the 1600s, and it seems her whereabouts were never discovered at the time. The remains

of a girl were discovered in the well, which is believed to have been the farmer's daughter, although the story behind how she died remains a mystery – was it suicide? Was she murdered? Was she accused of witchcraft? No one knows. The Nottingham psychic research team saw a ghost in this area; it rose up from the well, moved towards the hall then disappeared, which could have been the farmer's daughter, and there had been many similar reports of such a spirit in the past.

We now move onwards to the caretaker's office, which is believed to be the home of a poltergeist. There have been reports of the physical movement of objects here that are inexplicable. The current caretaker firmly believes his office to be haunted. One day, while he was sitting on the sofa with a colleague, a toilet roll launched itself off the shelf and landed in the middle of the room. This was a little surprising, but he picked it up sat back down and continued with the conversation, not thinking too much of it. Then a plastic cup holder flew from one side of the room and hit his colleague on the shoulder and rolled on to the floor. Both of these events are without a normal explanation, and it is simply not possible for the objects to have travelled that far simply by falling. In the same area an old gentleman has been seen, and the caretaker has seen him, too, walking through the tunnel nearby. He describes him as old and wearing a flat cap. There was no interaction between the two of them, which might suggest this was an apparition, and he just turned and disappeared. This caused such shock and fear that he would not go back in to the tunnel for two months afterwards.

Our next story is quite an horrific tale, resulting in a tragic and unnecessary death within the walls of the old hall. Mr Boothroyd, a horrible and revered man, was indecently assaulting a young girl in times when such things were not talked about, and the girl continued to suffer in silence at the hands of this hideous man. In her despair and suffering, she took her own life. Her dead body was found hanging from the staircase in the hall. The spirit of this girl is still in the castle, which is most probably because of the nature of her death, and she has been seen looking out from one of the windows, and there have been more eerie reports of choking noises coming from the room in which she died.

This is not the only story of suicide in Annesley Hall, there is another that I know of. A former member of staff was at a party at the hall when they ran out of champagne. He went outside to the owner's car to get out the extra case, which was parked on the driveway. As he turned around he saw someone standing in the window of the mews building, which was no longer in use. He turned, petrified, and ran back in to the house. He later discovered that the person he had seen was a woman, and she had appeared before other people working at the hall. The story behind the ghosts was that she had been a dairy maid at the hall sometime in the past. Servants lived above the station they worked in and she had apparently hanged herself there, although in this case the reasons why have been lost through time. She has also been heard shouting out for help – who knows whether they are cries of a changed mind of if the act was, in fact, carried out by someone else.

Would you believe even the clock here is haunted, and this tale is an experience I had myself here. In the clock tower sits an old Jonathon Whitehurst clock that has to be wound up once a week. The clock is dated 1767 and was made by a very reliable clock company based in Derby. Once wound, the clock has never been known to stop, but when I came here it stopped twice on request and this cannot possibly be explained by normal reasoning.

Inside the hall, the paranormal activity continues. The plethora of ghosts here is really remarkable. Among the rooms in what is now really just an empty shell, tales of love and hatred abound. In one of the rooms there was, at one time, a beautiful wooden staircase, and this is the scene of the next tragic death that we know of that occurred in Annesley Hall. In 1600 a maid went missing from the house, but no one knew what had happened to her, and in those days maids and servants were not important people so her whereabouts were never a great concern to anyone and she was soon forgotten. Until one day, that is, when electricity was being put in to the house, and the electricians had to dig under the stairs to lay the cables. Here they made a very grim and saddening discovery. They found the body of a young girl with a baby in her arms, buried here in unconsecrated ground. She had been stabbed and buried here to cover up this wicked deed. It is believed that she was that missing maid and there have being many sightings of her here, standing and holding up her arms as if cradling a baby. In the 1800s William Howatt, an Irish lad and a medium, stayed at the hall, and he felt the presence of two ghosts; one of them was a young girl cradling a baby in her arms in front of the fire.

I think the most frightening place at the hall has to be the cellar. There is a lot of evil connected to it from times when devil worshipping was carried out here, and this place has a dark and heavy atmosphere and an uncomfortable feeling that is quite overcoming. There is a legend that William Chaworth and the fifth Lord Byron fought a duel at the Star and Garter pub in London in 1765. It has been said that the duel was over pheasants and hares, but others believe it was over who would lead the ghastly group they had set up here, similar to a Hell Fire club. This is a story connecting negative energy with this place, and some believe William is one of the spirits that are haunting this cellar. Dead bodies were also laid out here on the cold concrete floor as it kept them cool before they were taken in to church and then buried, so who knows what spirits could lie here because of that. A figure has been seen here in military uniform and there have been lots of military people connected with the hall over the years that it has been habited.

There used to be a secret passageway that led out from the cellar, but this has now been filled in. It is believed that there is serious evil in the passageway, and when I was there I was advised very strongly not to try to dig it out in any way by a local medium, who has a strong sense of negative energy whenever she is here. Attempts have been made before, but bricks start to fall and all attempts have failed for fear of it caving in. Negative spirits here feed on negative energy that is created from people being afraid, and they continue to frighten all those brave enough to enter the cellars. It is believed that there is something elemental here and that it is getting stronger, and I am most afraid of this.

Back upstairs, in slightly less sinister surroundings, the paranormal activity continues – this time in relation to perhaps one of the most famous stories connected to the house: the story of Lord Byron and his childhood sweetheart Mary Chaworth. In the main hallway of the building, it is here that Lord Byron's hopes and aspirations were dashed by Mary when she was here talking to her cousin. Because of the acoustics, Lord Byron was able to hear the conversation as he rode up to the Annesley, and he overheard Mary say she would not be marrying Byron. He rode away devastated and heart broken as she was the love of his life. He went back to Newstead Abbey and didn't return for many years. Years later, Mary married Jack Musters, which turned out to be a very stormy marriage.

Lord Byron had inherited Newstead Abbey from his great uncle when he was 10 years old so had spent a lot of time at Annesley over the years. It is believed that both Mary and Lord Byron still haunt their bedrooms at the hall. Mary has been seen disappearing through a wall that used to be a French window that lead out on to her terrace, where she would eat breakfast on nice days. It is also believed that Mary's youngest son Charles haunts the place and has been reunited with his mother as he was her favourite child. This spirit, however, is not as serene as his mother and has thrown stones at people in this area. He died from swamp fever in South America at the same time that his mother was dying from rheumatic fever at home. He was a shipman aboard the HMS *Beagle* with Charles Darwin. When he died his chest containing his belongings was brought back to the hall and Jack Musters, his father, locked it up in the hallway and no one was allowed in for 6 months.

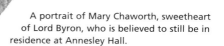

A portrait of Mary Chaworth, sweetheart of Lord Byron, who is believed to still be in residence at Annesley Hall.

The impressive Annesley Hall, home of evil spirits in its dark cellars.

When Byron died, Mary was shielded from the truth in order to protect her. However, it was his wish to have a funeral procession around Newstead Abbey and Annesley Hall and this was carried out. Mary was sitting on the terrace on this very day, and she saw the procession on its journey. She immediately enquired to her staff what it was for, and one naïve new servant let it slip that it was actually the funeral procession of her childhood sweetheart. She was distraught and immediately ordered everyone off the terrace, and as they turned to walk away they saw the tears begin to roll down here cheeks, welling up with grief.

2 2

THE GALLERIES
OF JUSTICE

The original site of Nottinghamshire County Gaol is not known, but it may well have been within Nottingham Castle, perhaps in its sandstone dungeons. The first mention of a county gaol is in a charter of Henry VI in 1449 '...our messuage called the Kings Hall wherin is our gaol for the counties of Nottingham and Derby...'

The Shire Hall and gaol were of course two different units. The Shire or County Hall was the Kings Hall for here the king's local representative, the sheriff, upheld and represented the king in the county. There is evidence that ... 'a hall of the Lord King ...' was on the site from 1375.

Rarely has a County Hall and gaol remained on the same site for so long. It is also quite unique for a felon to be tried, imprisoned and executed on the same site. It is also unique for the original cells, dungeons, courts and mediaeval caves still to be preserved. No wonder there are so many tormented souls still haunting the building.

During the period 1770–1830, known as the Bloody Cod, there were well over 200 hanging offences in Britain. You name it you could be hanged for it. Digging up turnips setting fire to haystacks, stealing a sheep, shopbreaking, housebreaking, forgery, poaching and appearing on the streets with a sooty face were all hanging offences. So many unfortunate wretches were executed here for very trivial offences.

Why should the Galleries of Justice be so haunted? People die everywhere! It's the conditions in which they die. Until the 1870s most hanged people died of slow strangulation, kicking writhing, choking and vomiting in front of their family, friends, and neighbours, as all executions in this country were held in public until 1868. If you had a few bob you could pay the hangman to quicken your end by climbing the ladder and standing on your shoulders – not a pretty sight.

You could be hanged for murder but also for stealing a sheep. The punishment was increased for murderers with public dissection or gibbeting after death. This was playing with the minds of ignorant but religious people. They would not, of course, have a decent burial in consecrated ground. The body would not be whole and, therefore, the soul would not be whole and when the last trumpet was blown they would be condemned to eternal damnation and burn in hell.

For the last 2,000 years the church ruled by fear: commit crimes and you will go to hell. Most of the people who passed through the portals of the Galleries of Justice considered themselves sinners and would not be allowed into heaven. Therefore, they would choose to stay earthbound and haunt the place where they died rather than face rejection outside the Pearly Gates by St Peter.

It is always difficult with very haunted properties to tell whether one spirit is creating all the activity or if there is more than one entity within the building. With the Galleries, there have been so many sightings of different figures and some are seen so regularly that they are recognisable to the staff.

In the entrance hall a man in Victorian dress, a lady and a soldier have been seen, as well as frequent cold spots being experienced. In one of the courts terrible sighs and groans are heard as well as dark figures being witnessed. In the corridors of the gaol, doors slam footsteps are heard and keys rattle in long-gone cell doors. The laundry room is particularly haunted, by a woman who is often seen by staff and visitors alike. Strange smells are experienced and doors open and shut on their own. The exercise yard, unconsecrated of course, houses the shade of a young man who disappears through the wall. This area is where many executed felons and suicides would have found their last resting place, but ARE THEY TRULY AT REST?

The Shire Hall pictured in 1990.

23

COLWICK HALL

There has been a settlement on the site of Colwick Hall certainly since Saxon times. The hall that you see today was built in 1776 by Samuel Stretton. Many years before, the hall was surrounded by a deep moat accessed by a drawbridge on the north side of the property. This deep moat was a cause of much consternation and many disputes between the inhabitants of Colwick and the neighbours, as it required so much water to keep it full.

In 1362, on the death of William Colwick, the property passed to another family by the marriage of his daughter into the Byron Family. They lived there for over 100 years before it came into the possession of the Musters family, quite ironic as Mary Chaworth-Musters was the childhood sweetheart and only true love of the poet Lord Byron.

Much to the dismay of Byron, Mary Chaworth married Jack Musters, 'The fox hunting squire' from Colwick Hall. For many years they lived at Annesley Hall, but in 1827 on the death of old John Musters, Jack's father, they moved in to Colwick. Mary must have missed Annesley, which had been her home since she was born. The furniture and all the furnishings were alien to her as the beautiful, stately Sophia Musters, Jacks mother who had died eight years earlier, had chosen them all. It was Sophia who had painted the beautiful window on the stairs. Portraits of the Musters family stared down at Mary from the walls, and she believed that the hall was haunted by her mother in law, Sophia.

Mary always felt uneasy there and the faces of the tenants were those of strangers and not like those of her beloved tenants from Annesley. She did not like the furtive looks on some of the gaunt faces, which she saw when she travelled into nearby Nottingham. She was only too well aware that they resented her for being so wealthy when they were so desperately poor.

These poor Nottinghamshire folk were soon to cause uproar in the Chaworth-Musters household. Poaching was increasing as the people became hungrier; many of them worked in gangs and would stop at nothing, including the murder of any gamekeepers who got in their way. The war between them and the landed gentry was becoming increasingly violent. The Musters were known to have used mantraps and spring guns on Colwick land. Mantraps could seriously maim someone, but spring guns loaded with ball or shot could kill. No one knows how many poachers died in the woods or dragged themselves home to die, or how many children wandering onto the land fell foul of Jack Musters, until both contraptions were abolished in 1827.

The gap between rich and poor was getting wider after the black act was introduced, creating over 200 hanging offences. Nottinghamshire was in a state of unrest, and the

16th-century Colwick Hall, believed by some to be haunted by the ghost of Mary Chaworth.

slightest incident could cause a riot. In 1831 the riots came when the Reform Bill was thrown out of the House of Lords. There was big trouble in Bristol and Derby, and in Nottingham the rioters burnt down the castle and then moved on to Colwick. They attacked the hall and broke in, smashing furniture and pictures as they rampaged through the house. Mary was hiding in the ballroom with her daughter and a Swiss friend, Mademoiselle de Fey. When the rioters set fire to the place the women fled into the garden and hid in the shrubbery under the thick laurels, although it was now dark and raining heavily. After stealing many valuables the rioters eventually left, but the house was uninhabitable and the three unfortunate ladies had to sleep in the stables.

Mary never recovered from that traumatic ordeal and died not long afterwards of rheumatic fever.

There is the ghost of a young lady who haunts the hall and the grounds of Colwick Hall; many say it is the ghost of Mary

The impressive stone church in the grounds of Colwick Hall, a place steeped in history.

Chaworth-Musters. Others believe it to be the ghost of her mother in law, who loved the place so much and left such an impression on the building. Others claim that it is the ghost of Mademoiselle de Fey who, during her flight from the burning house, lost a case of jewels and a very valuable pearl necklace. They say that her restless ghost is still searching both house and grounds looking for her beloved necklace.

When I visited the hall I was told by many members of the staff that most of the rooms, including the attics, were haunted. At the time they had a parrot in reception that was forever staring into a corner and talking to someone that no human eyes could see. They told me that the grounds and also the ruined church yard were also haunted, possibly by the unfortunate Mary Chaworth-Musters who lies restless still waiting for her beloved Byron while surrounded by so many of his early ancestors. I went there at the request of Central Television to view a photo of the ghostly lady of Colwick, standing in front of a full-length mirror. It's quite impressive, but is it Sophia Musters, Mademoiselle de Fey or Mary Chaworth-Musters? Perhaps one day we will find out.

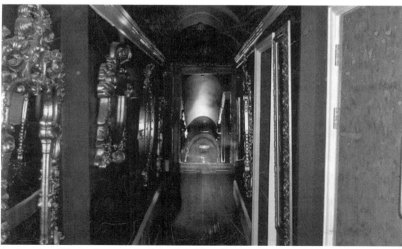

Captured on film, a photograph of the Colwick Hall ghost.

24

RUFFORD ABBEY

The 12th-century Rufford Abbey is set in a beautiful country park with areas of wood and parkland. It was founded by Cistercian monks and is now widely believed to be haunted by some of its former residents. The Cistercian order followed very strict religious beliefs and lead a simple life. The abbey was closed in 1536 after the Dissolution of the Monasteries and was very run down by then due to the poverty of its resident monks and lack of people willing to join the order. The abbey then passed to the hands of a rich and powerful family, the Talbots. It was transformed in to a beautiful country house and remained with the family until 1626. It then passed in to the hands of the Savile family from Yorkshire, who lived at Rufford until 1938. Many changes have been made to the old buildings over the years.

Many ghosts stories and legends have been told through the years: a White Lady glides through the ruins and an old lady in a black dress has been seen drifting around the grounds, maybe former residents of the abbey. But a more horrifying story is that of a murder that took place here and has left its mark on the old building. A child was killed here in one of the bedrooms after she was caught trying to run away from her attacker. The child attempted to hide under one of the huge four-poster beds, but it was no use. Her

What is left of Rufford Abbey, still haunted by the Cistercian monks who founded it.

The inside of the Abbey where a White Lady glides through.

screams must have echoed around the rooms as her life was cruelly taken. No one knows why or who was responsible for this treacherous deed, but guests to the former abbey have reported feeling a small child nestling against them and shivering, waking them in the middle of the night.

Another even more frightening tale is that of the Black Friar. It is described as a huge figure with a death's head under its cowl and has been seen in mirrors and also taps the shoulders of unsuspecting guests. The burial register at Edwinstowe Church even records the death of a local man that had a run in with the Black Friar, who is reported as dying from fright after the terrifying meeting in the 20th century.

Rufford Abbey is reported to be the home of a terrifying Black Friar.

FURTHER
RESEARCH

If you have been caught by the ghost-hunting bug after reading about our adventures in Nottinghamshire, the following publications and DVDs may be of interest to you.

Books:

The Ghost Tour of Great Britain: Derbyshire with Richard Felix, Breedon Books, 2005.

The Ghost Tour of Great Britain: Wales with Richard Felix, Breedon Books, 2005.

The Ghost Tour of Scotland: with Richard Felix, Breedon Books, 2006.

The Ghost Tour of Yorkshire: with Richard Felix, Breedon Books, 2005.

The Ghost Tour of Lincolnshire: with Richard Felix, Breedon Books, 2006.

The above books are available from all good bookshops and may also be purchased direct from the publishers, Breedon Books, 3 The Parker Centre, Mansfield Road, Derby, DE21 4SZ, tel 01332 384235, fax 01332 292755, email sales@breedonpublishing.co.uk.

DVDs

This DVDs, as well as many others from the Ghost Tour of Great Britain, are available from shops in Derby and direct from the producers, Films Factory, 61 Mill Lane, Belper, DE56 1LH, tel 01773 880620. Order online at: www.filmsfactory.co.uk

INDEX